Twenty-Seven Bible Crosswords

by

Dr. Bernard Kent, Jr.

Cover Design: SOS Graphics and Designs

Published by G Publishing, LLC
P. O. Box 24374
Detroit, MI 48224

ISBN 13: 978-0-9823533-3-2
10: 0-9823533-3-2

Library of Congress Control Number: 2009901241

Printed in the United States of America

Acknowledgement

A special thanks goes to my son Absolon (Al) for his hard work and support. He spent many hours editing and typing each page to make sure all of the work was included and completed.

Son, I want you to know I appreciate your love and confidence to assist with this work.

Love you very much.
Dad.

Matthew

ACROSS

2. Number of generations from Abraham to Christ (two-word answer)
5. Father of David
6. Key word to the Scribe and Pharisees
8. Birthplace of Jesus
10. Fortieth book of the Bible
12. First missing word in phrase, "No one can serve _______ ________"
13. Last missing word in phrase, "No one can serve _______ ________"
14. Said, "There is no resurrection"
16. Jesus said, "My house shall be called a house of ____________"
17. That Jesus Christ is the son of David is the book's central _____________
19. The wife of this man ________ asked for a special seat in the kingdom for his sons
20. Betrayer (two-word answer)

DOWN

1. Highest standard above Jewish Legalism was _________ _________ (two-word answer)
3. Number of years the woman had the blood problem
4. Denied Jesus
7. In this book , the phrase "the kingdom of heaven" is used _________ _________ times (two-word answer)
9. __________ your enemies
11. Matthew's occupation (two-word answer)
13. Jesus discussed the end of time at this place with the disciples (three-word answer)
15. Last word in the book
18. The _________said "Lord, I am not worthy that you should come to my house."

Matthew

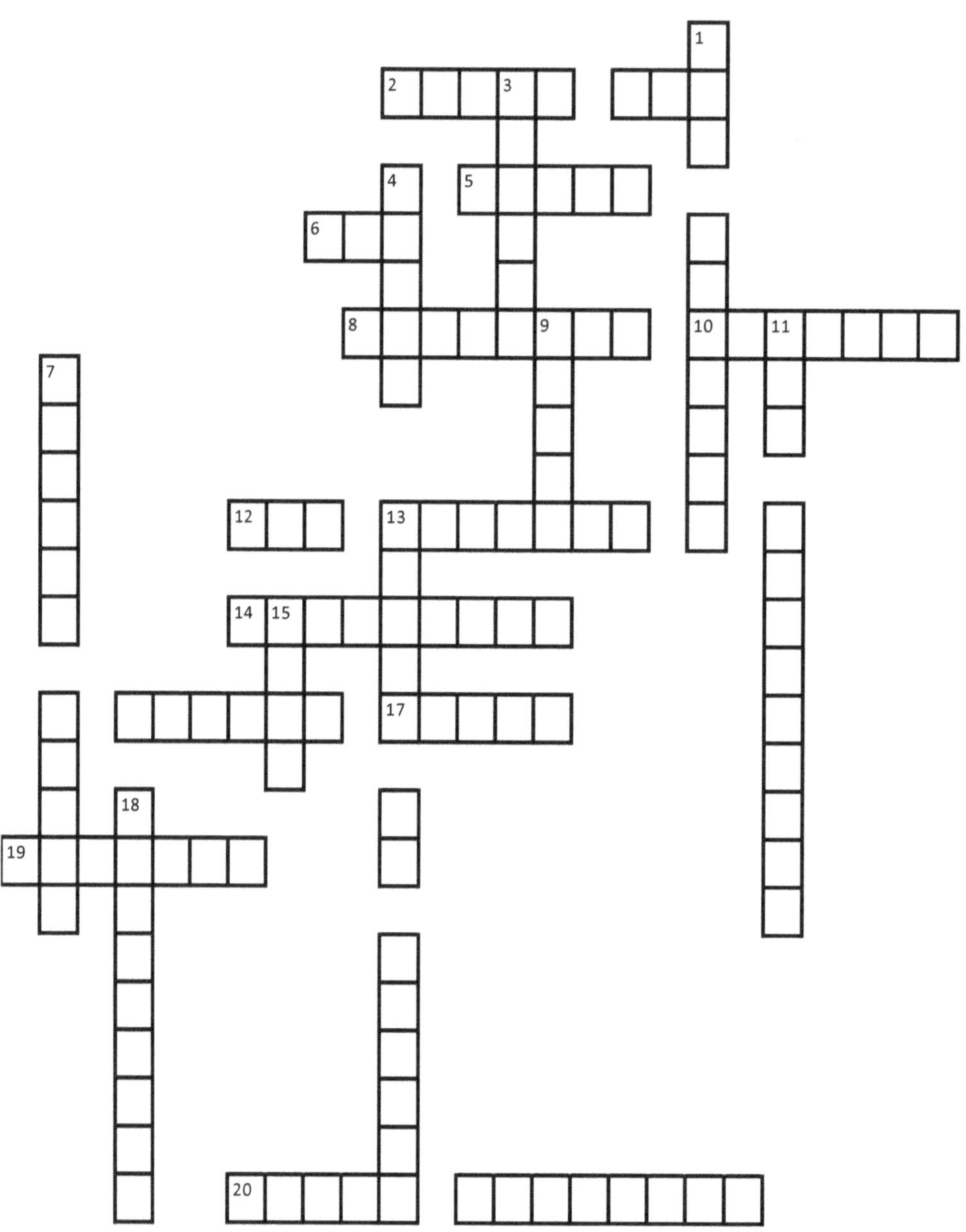

Mark

ACROSS

2. Forty-first book of the Bible
3. Jesus cleansed the ___________of money changers
4. A prisoner
7. Mark is one of the three _______ gospels
9. Jesus was buried in ________'s tomb
12. This unseeing character said "Jesus, son of David, have mercy on me" (two-word answer)
16. Stated "There is no resurrection."
17. Translated, it means "place of the skull"

DOWN

1. Father of James and John
2. Mother of Jesus
3. Number of disciples
5. A garden
6. "I will make your enemies your ___________"
8. Taxes were paid to____________
9. A betrayer (two-word answer)
10. Jesus healed a man with a withered hand on the_____________
11. Denied Jesus
13. Jesus cleansed a____________
14. John preached a baptism of __________
15. Jesus was baptized by John in the ___________ river.

Mark

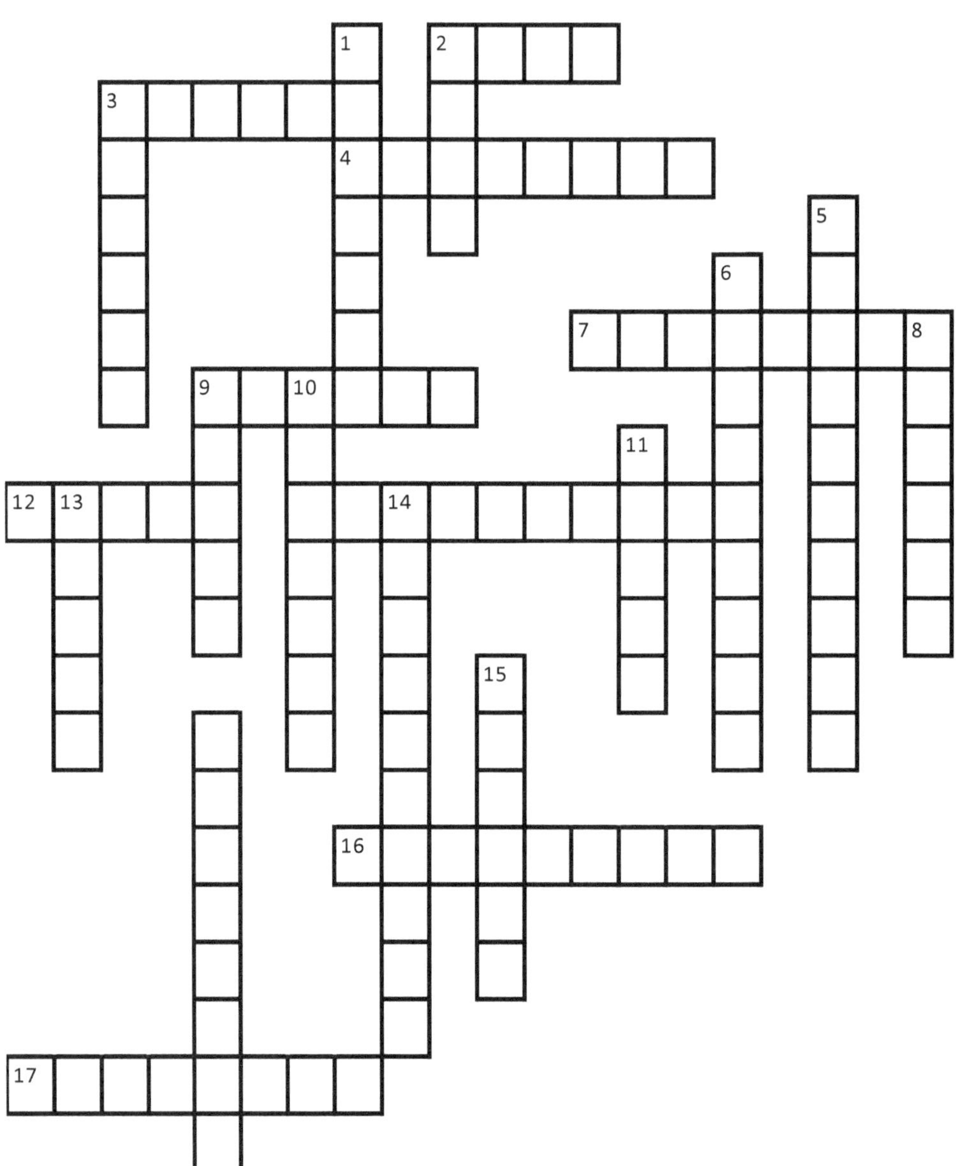

Luke

ACROSS

2. Forced to carry the cross of Jesus
3. Name shouted by a blind man (three-word answer)
4. "Suffer little ________ to come unto me, and forbid them not"
5. City of David
7. A beggar
8. Hebrew place of worship
9. Name for the Feast of Unleavened Bread
10. Received a revelation to see Jesus before his death
12. Wife of Zacharius the priest
15. Jesus beheld Jerusalem and _____over it
17. Governor of Judea (two-word answer)
18. Angel sent by God to Galilee

DOWN

1. After Jesus faced Herod, this person became Herod's friend
3. Denied that there is a resurrection
6. Forty-second book of the Bible
10. Ten Lepers were told to show themselves to the ____________
11. King of Judea
13. Gave two mites to the treasury
14. Jesus came here for the Feast of Passover
16. Peter ___________Jesus three times

Luke

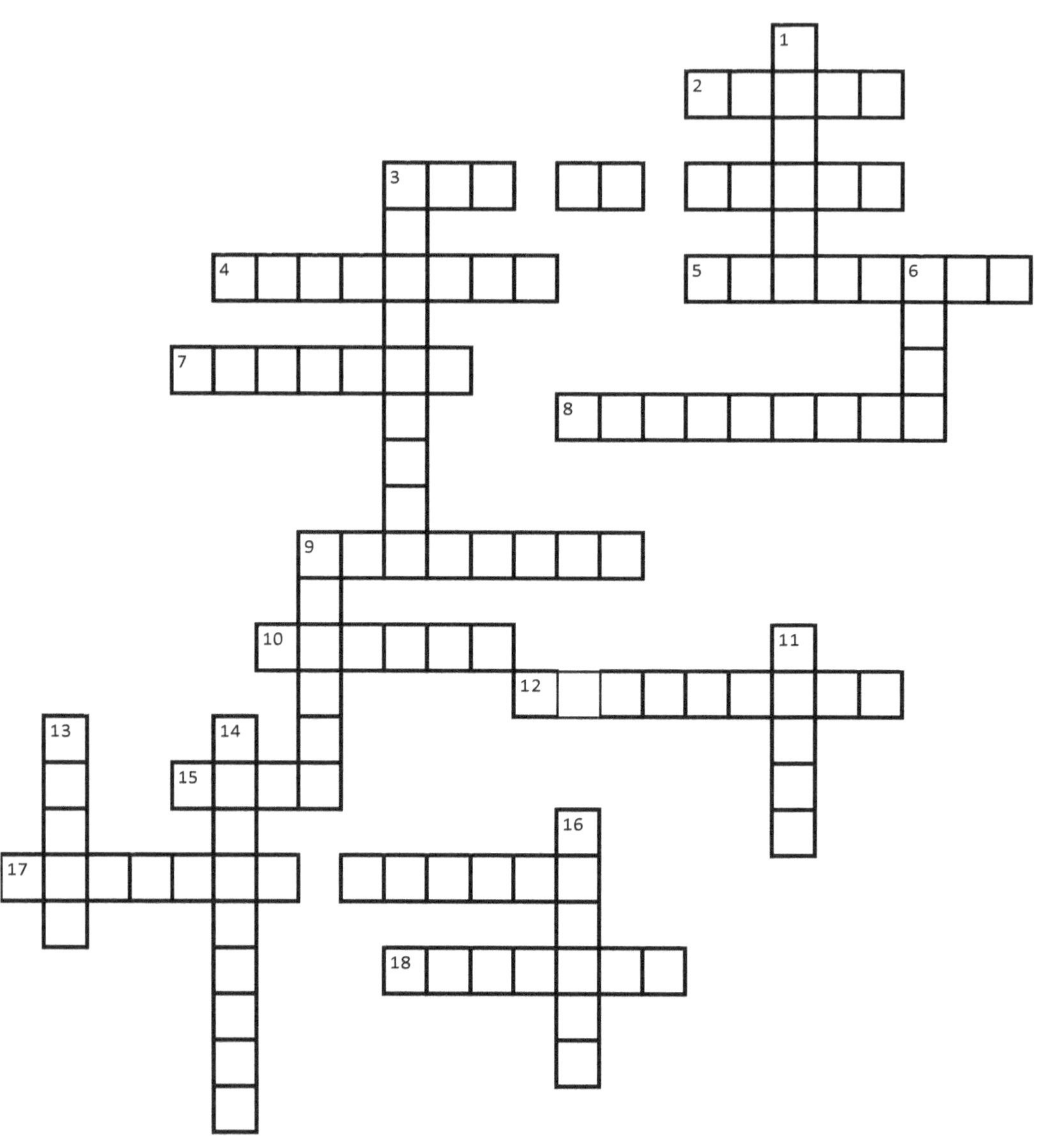

John

ACROSS

5. Had five husbands (two-word answer)

7. Brother of Mary and Martha

11. The truth shall make you_________

12. Jesus said "I am the _______of the world"

13. Forty third book of the Bible

15. Philip, Andrew, and Peter were from this city.

16. Another name for the Sea of Galilee (three-word answer)

17. A new commandment (three-word answer)

19. Son of Simon (two-word answer)

20. High priest

DOWN

1. She went to an empty tomb (two-word answer)

2. "If anyone thirst, let them come to me and ___________"

3. The triumphal entry into Jerusalem was greeted with this word

4. Disciple of Jesus

6. A ruler of the Jews

8. "I am the good ___________

9. Stated "I find no fault in him"

10. In the beginning was the ________

14. At a wedding in Cana, water was turned to ____________

18. To him, seeing is believing

John

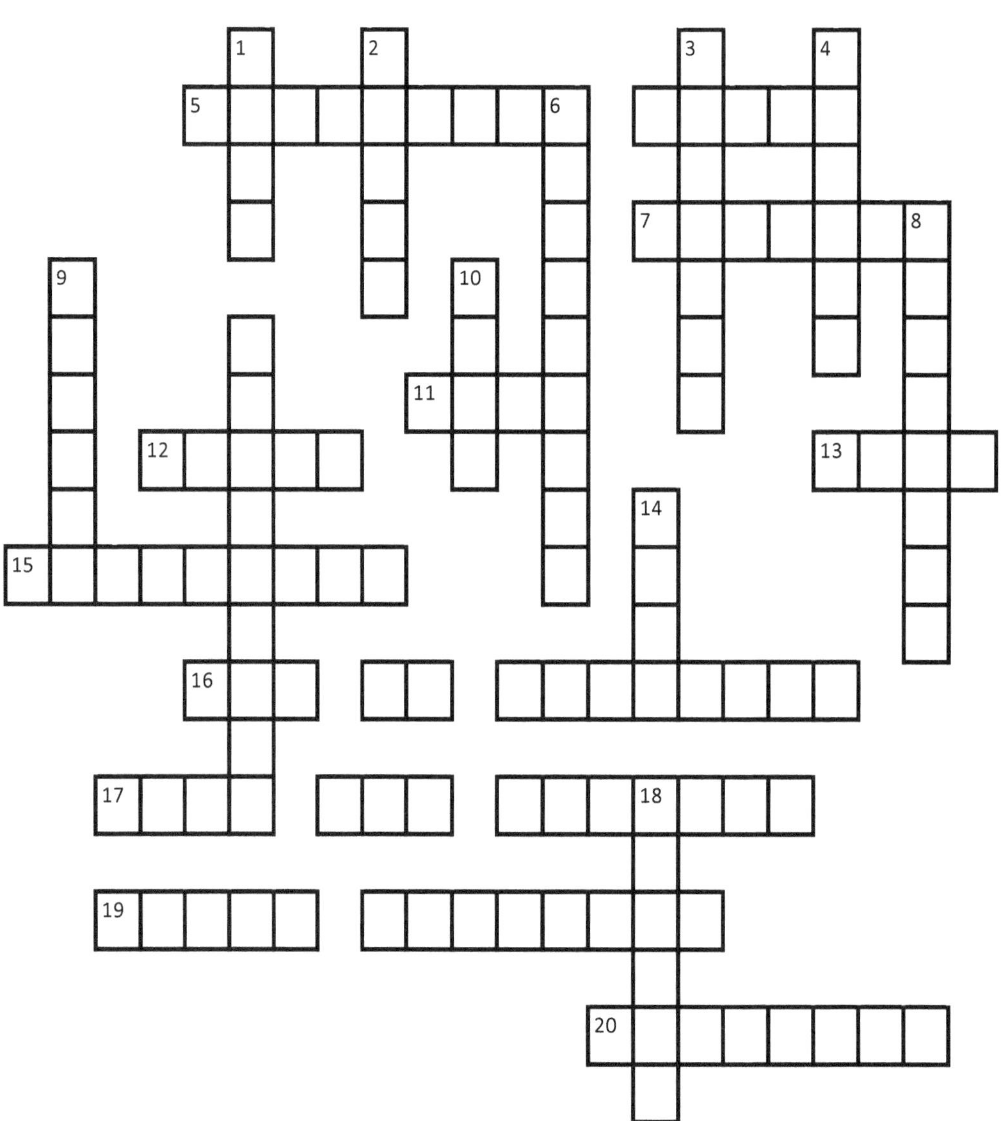

Acts

ACROSS

2. Philip baptized an______________

4. Place where God appeared to Saul with a light (two-word answer)

7. Stated "Lord do not charge them with this sin"

8. Characteristic of Peter and James

10. A member in the upper room

11. Saul's new name

13. A just centurion

16. King who killed James the brother of Jesus

17. Highest Jewish tribunal

19. A great persecutor of the church

20. Place where Paul was arrested

DOWN

1. A good woman restored to life

3. Paul disagreed with ______over John Mark.

5. A man who fell dead for lying

6. Forty-fourth book of the Bible

8. Sorcerer and false prophet

9. "Ye shall be witness" is the ________ ________ of Acts (two-word answer)

12. How you should never write God's name (abbreviation)

14. A riot occurred here

15. Came on the Day of Pentecost (two-word answer)

18. A Jew who was born at Alexandria

Acts

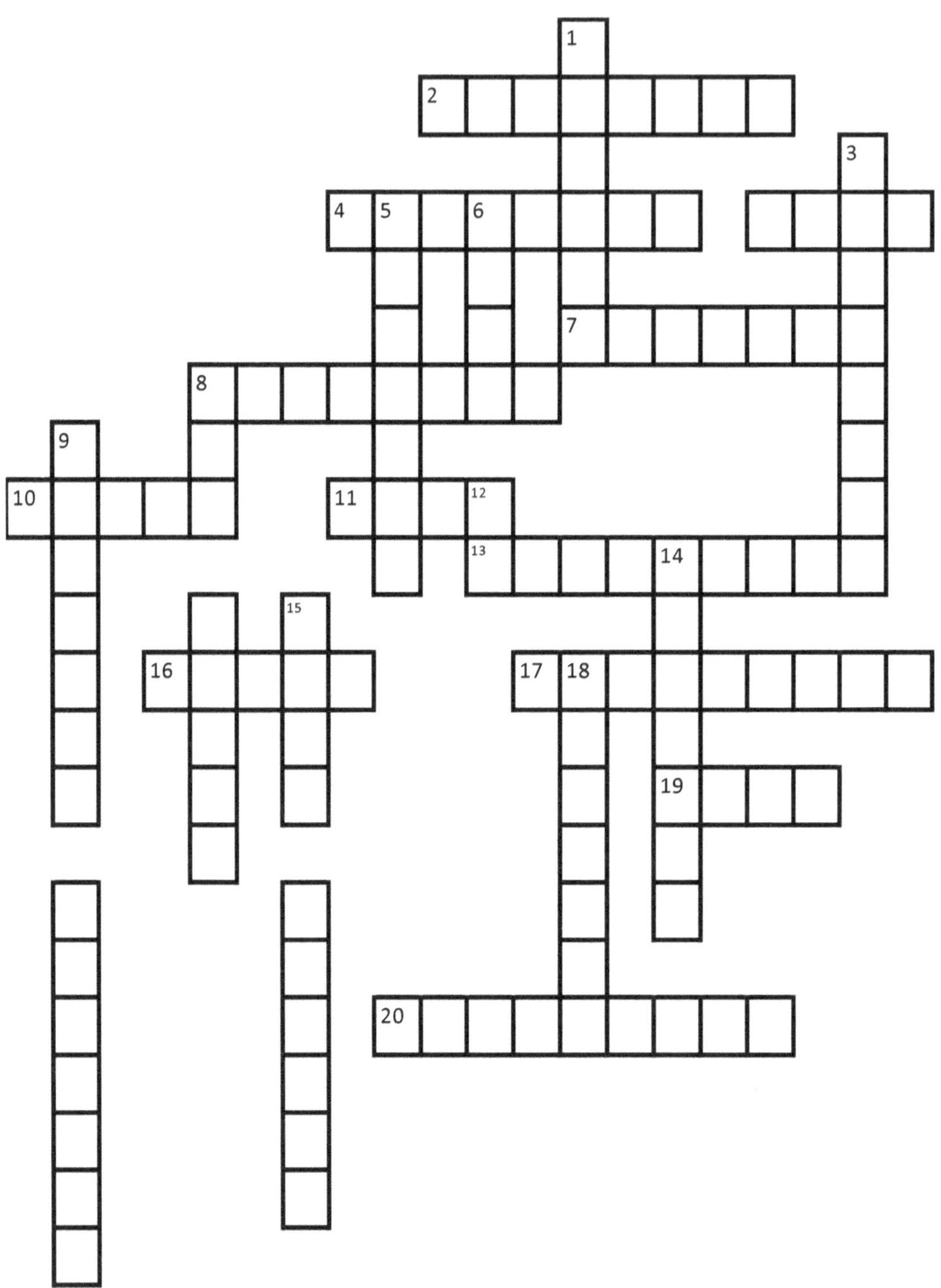

Romans

ACROSS

3. Father of many nations
4. All have _______________
5. Author of Romans
7. The just shall live by __________
12. For the wages of sin is __________
14. Do not be ________to this world
15. If God is for us, who can be against _____?

DOWN

1. Deliverance or salvation
2. While we were sinners, ________died for our sins
6. Owe no one anything except to _______ one another
8. For I am not _______of the gospel
9. Love without _____________
10. There is no _______to those who are in Christ Jesus
11. Forty-fifth book of the Bible
13. Do not let sin reign in your _______ body.

Romans

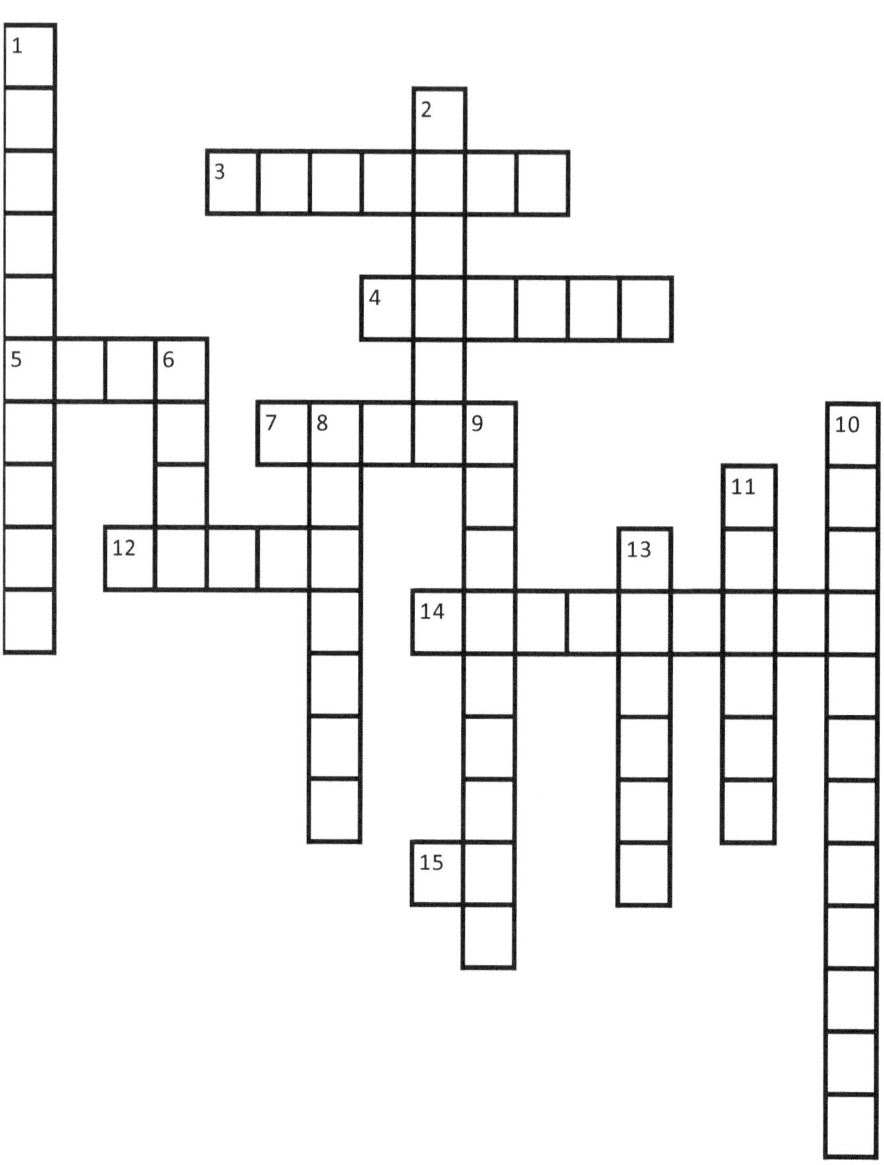

First Corinthians

ACROSS

7. Forty-sixth book of the Bible (two-word answer)

8. Love suffers long and is ________

10. There are diversities of gifts, but the same ________

11. Let all things be done for________

13. Let all that you do be done with ________

15. "I am of ________________"

18. For by one spirit, we were all baptized into one ____________

DOWN

1. When I became a man, I put away _______things

2. All things are lawful, but not all things __________

3. "Do this in ________ of me

4. Sin city

5. Oh death, where is your________?

6. The ___________will not inherit the Kingdom of God

9. The natural man does not receive the things of the __________ (three-word answer)

10. For the unbelieving husband is _______ by the wife

11. Love does not ________

12. Aquila and ___________

14. There is no other God but ________

16. The _______will judge the world

17. "Take, eat, this is my ________which was broken for you"

First Corinthians

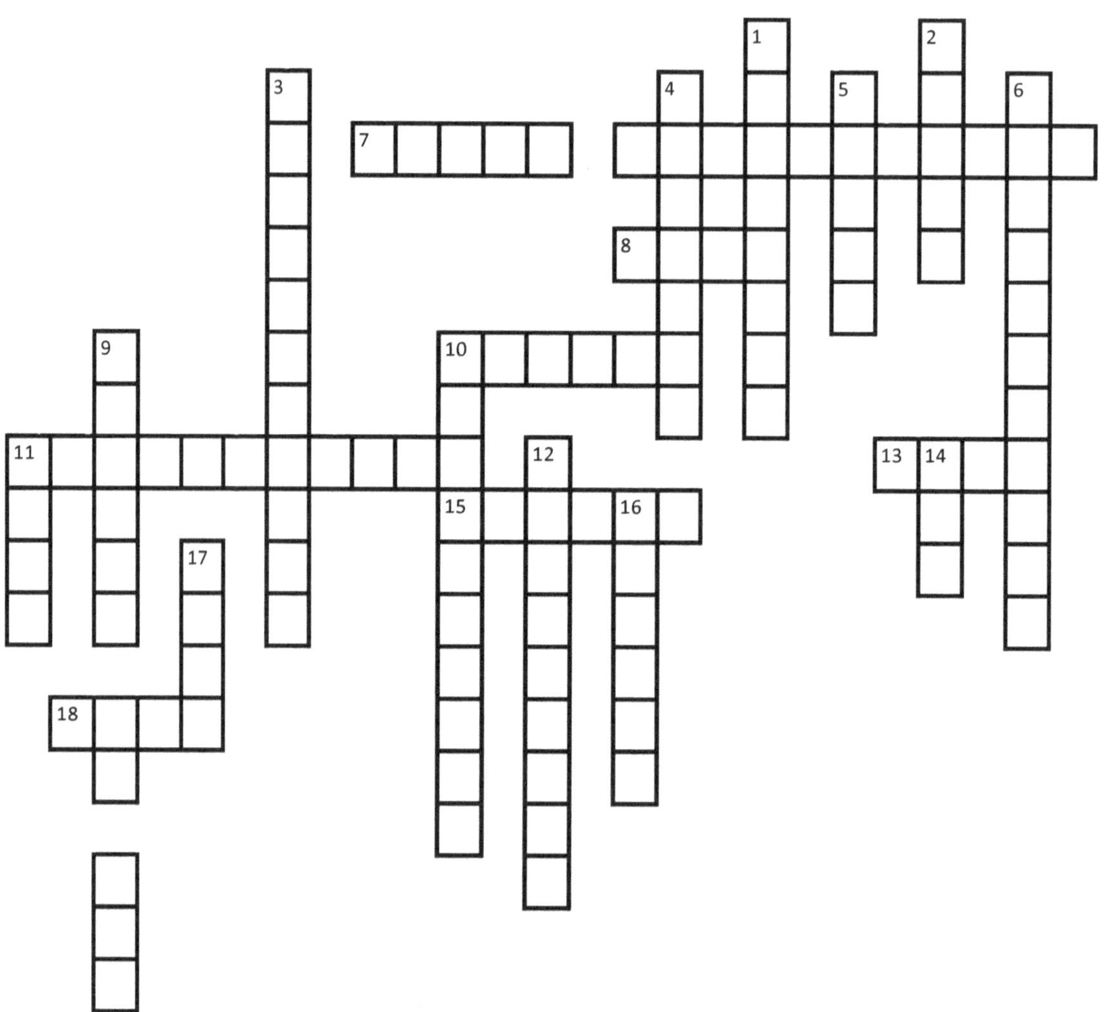

Second Corinthians

ACROSS

1. Forty-seventh book of the Bible

5. He who sows sparingly will reap
____

6. Where the spirit of the Lord is, there is
____

7. We are hard-pressed on every side, yet not ____________

9. Word for Holy Spirit

DOWN

2. The words comfort and________are used ten times in Chapter 1:3-7.

3. Enough

4. "My __________ is sufficient."

7. If any is in Christ, he is a new
____

8. Do not be unequally yoked with
____

Second Corinthians

Galatians

ACROSS

3. The Lord's brother

5. Paul rebuked __________

6. Bear one another's ___________

8. For 15 _______, Paul stayed with Peter in Jerusalem

12. What Galatians 5:1-5 is to the entire book of Galatians (two-word answer)

DOWN

1. It is no longer I who live, but Christ _________ in me

2. Forty-eighth book of the Bible

4. Paul's apostleship came from _________ ___________

6. Paul traveled to Jerusalem with ____________

7. Paul considered himself a __________ of Christ

9. You shall love your neighbor as _________

10. ___________in the spirit

11. You are sons of God through ______ in Jesus Christ

Galatians

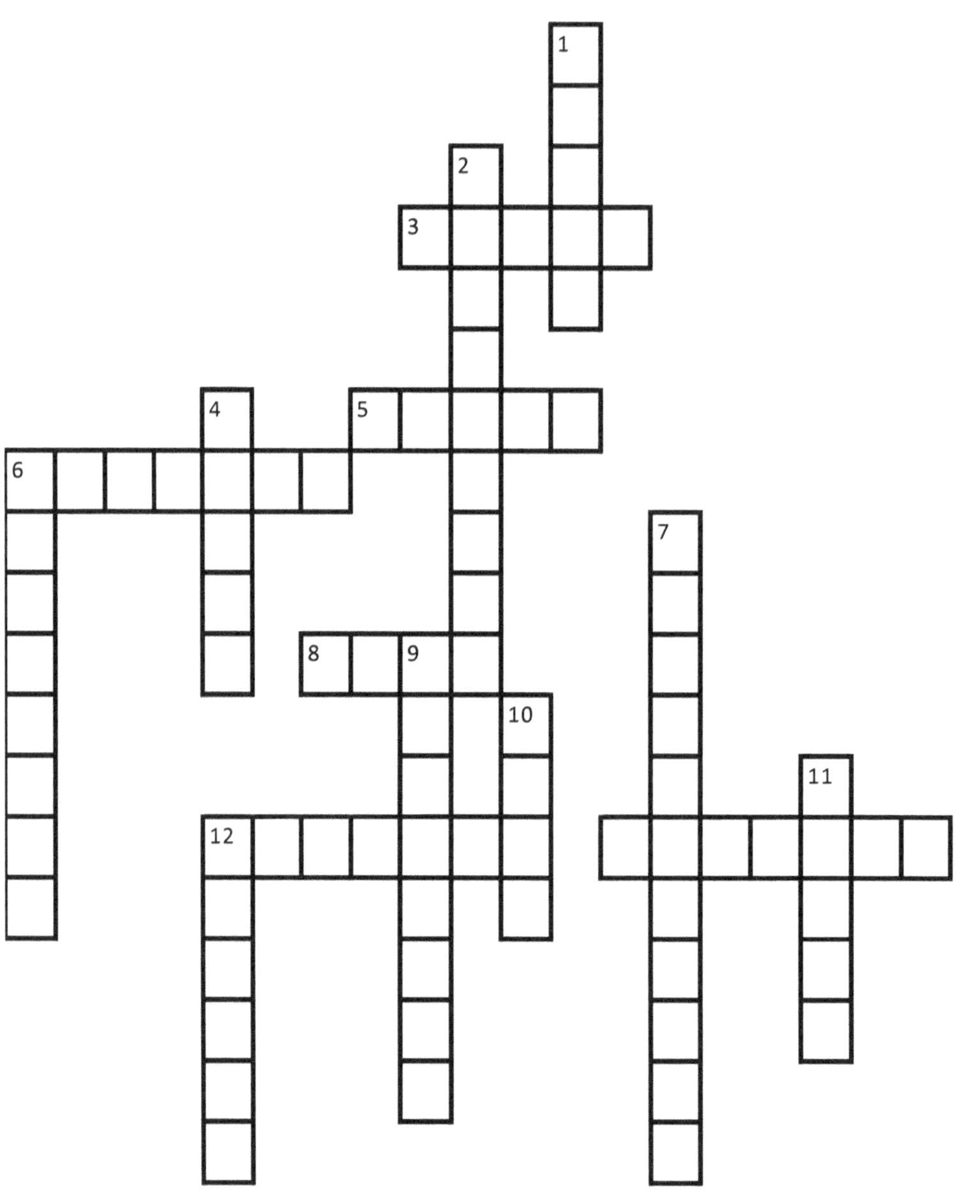

Ephesians

ACROSS

3. Be ____________ of God as dear children
4. _________, obey your parents in the Lord
6. Number of chapters in this book
9. Walk as children of _________
10. "I am Paul, the ___________ of Christ
12. God is rich in _____________
14. "Be angry and do not _________"
15. Book was written to the people of __________

DOWN

1. Be _________ to one another
2. Put on the whole _____________
5. Wives, love your ____________
7. Husbands, love your __________
8. Same as 12 Across (God has a lot of it)
11. There is _________ body and ______ spirit (two-word answer)
13. Forty-ninth book of the Bible

Ephesians

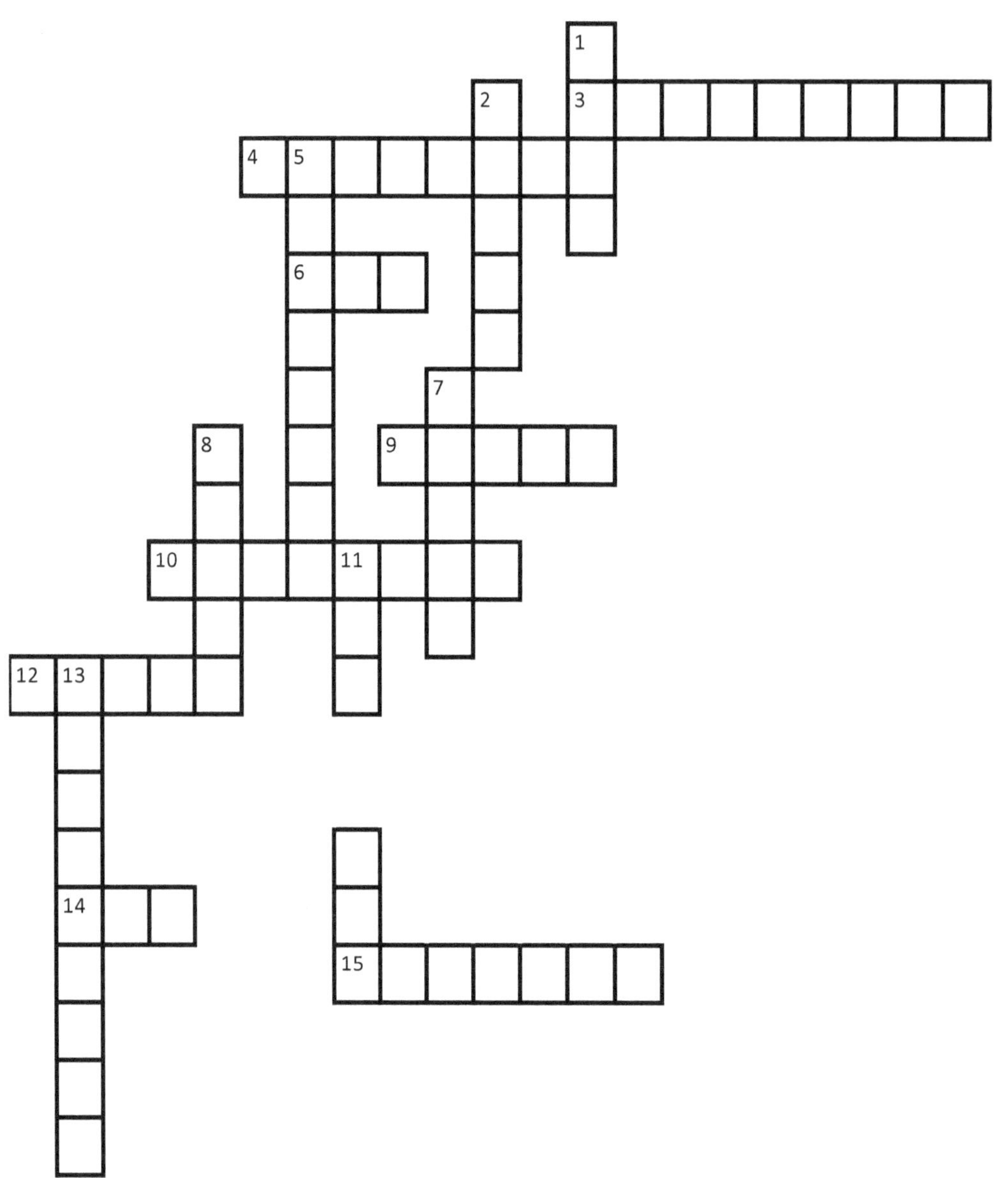

Philippians

ACROSS

2. Do all things without __________

3. I can do all things through Christ which _________ me.

8. "Be anxious for _____________"

8. Paul was a prisoner in ____________

9. Paul received aid from the church while in__________

DOWN

1. "______________those things which are behind"

4. For me to live in Christ, and to die is ____________

5. Fiftieth book of the Bible

6. "Beware of ____________. Beware of evil workers"

7. "But my God shall supply all your _________"

Philippians

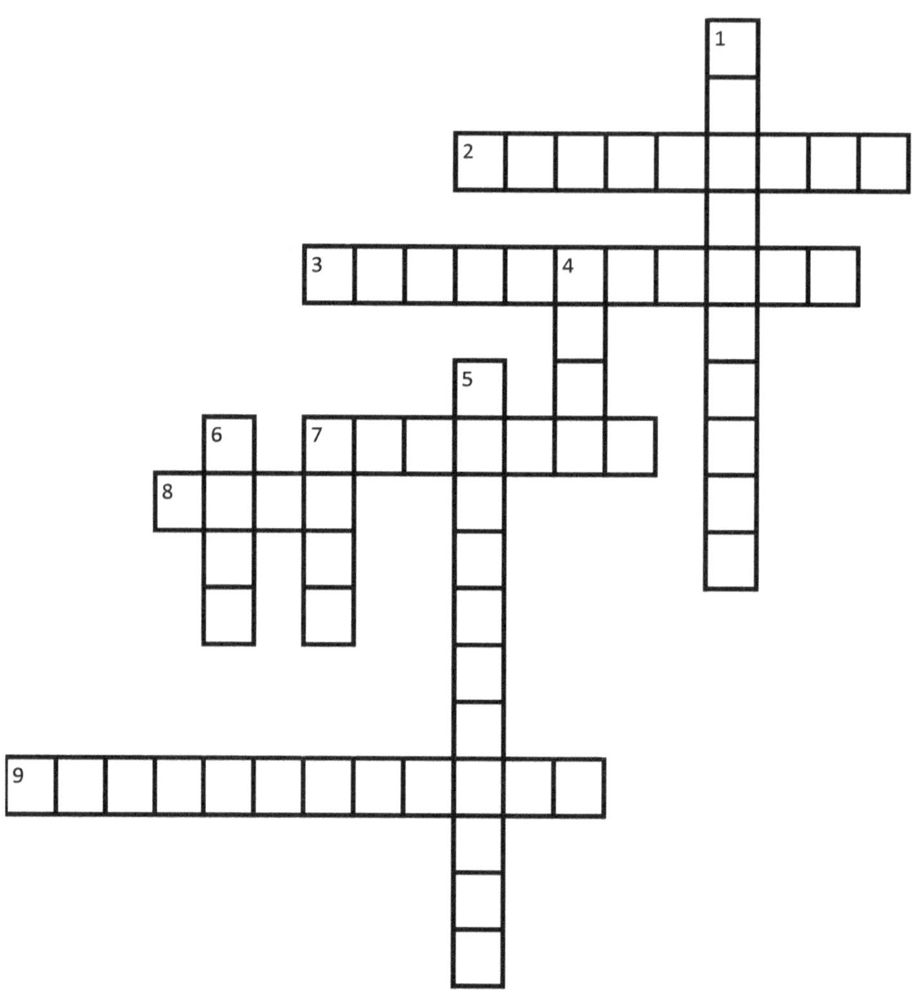

Colossians

ACROSS

3. Took Paul's letter to Colosse
4. Physician and author of Luke and Acts
5. Paul never visited this place. (Chapter 2, Verse 1)
10. A fellow prisoner with Paul
11. Runaway slave of Philemon

DOWN

1. Set your affection on things ______
2. Paul's fellow laborer in Rome, where he wrote his Epistle to the Colossians
5. Fifty-first book of the Bible
6. __________, love your wives
7. __________, submit to your husbands
8. __________,do not provoke your children
9. Cousin of Mark

Colossians

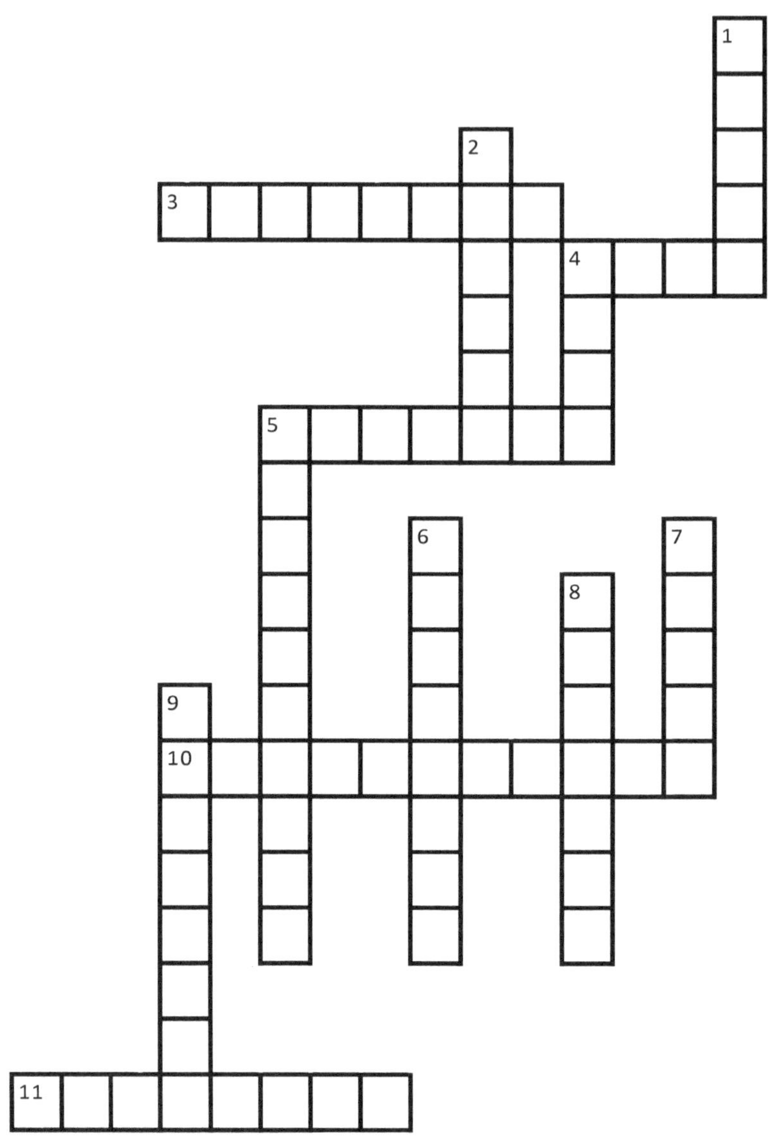

First Thessalonians

ACROSS

1. Co-worker with Paul
3. ____________without ceasing
6. Edify one _______________
7. Abstain from every form of ________
8. Fifty-second book of the Bible (two-word answer)
9. Paul and his companions were treated harshly at ___________
10. In everything give ___________

DOWN

2. Quench not the ____________
4. Be at _____________
5. Salutation

First Thessalonians

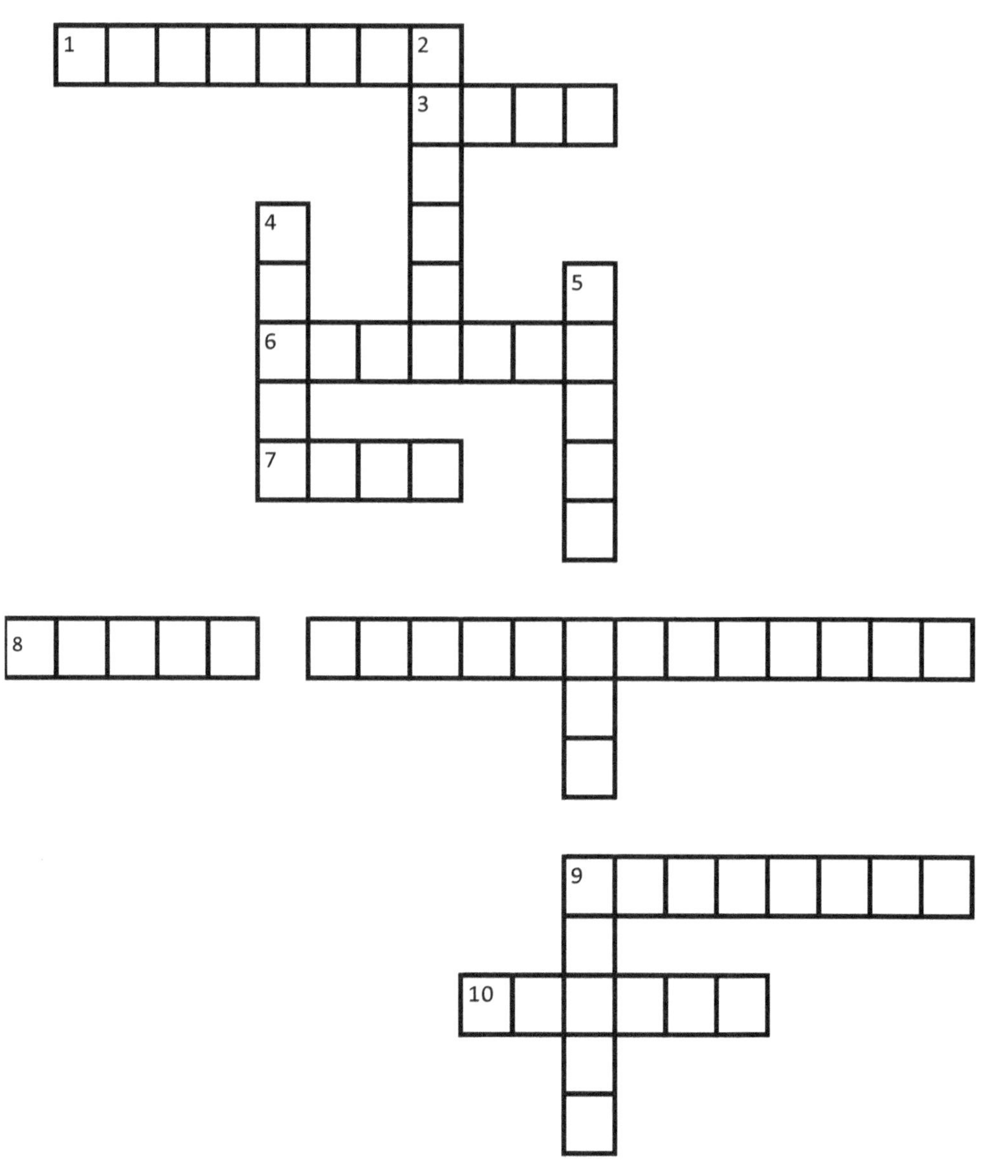

Second Thessalonians

ACROSS

3. The one whom the Lord will destroy

4. If anyone will not work, neither shall he__________

6. Co-worker with Paul

8. Central message (two-word answer)

9. The Lord is _______________

DOWN

1. Fifty-third book of the Bible (two-word answer)

2. The people of the church were being _________

3. Do not keep company with anyone that does not obey the ___________

5. Do not grow weary in doing _______

7. ____________ patiently for the coming of the Lord

Second Thessalonians

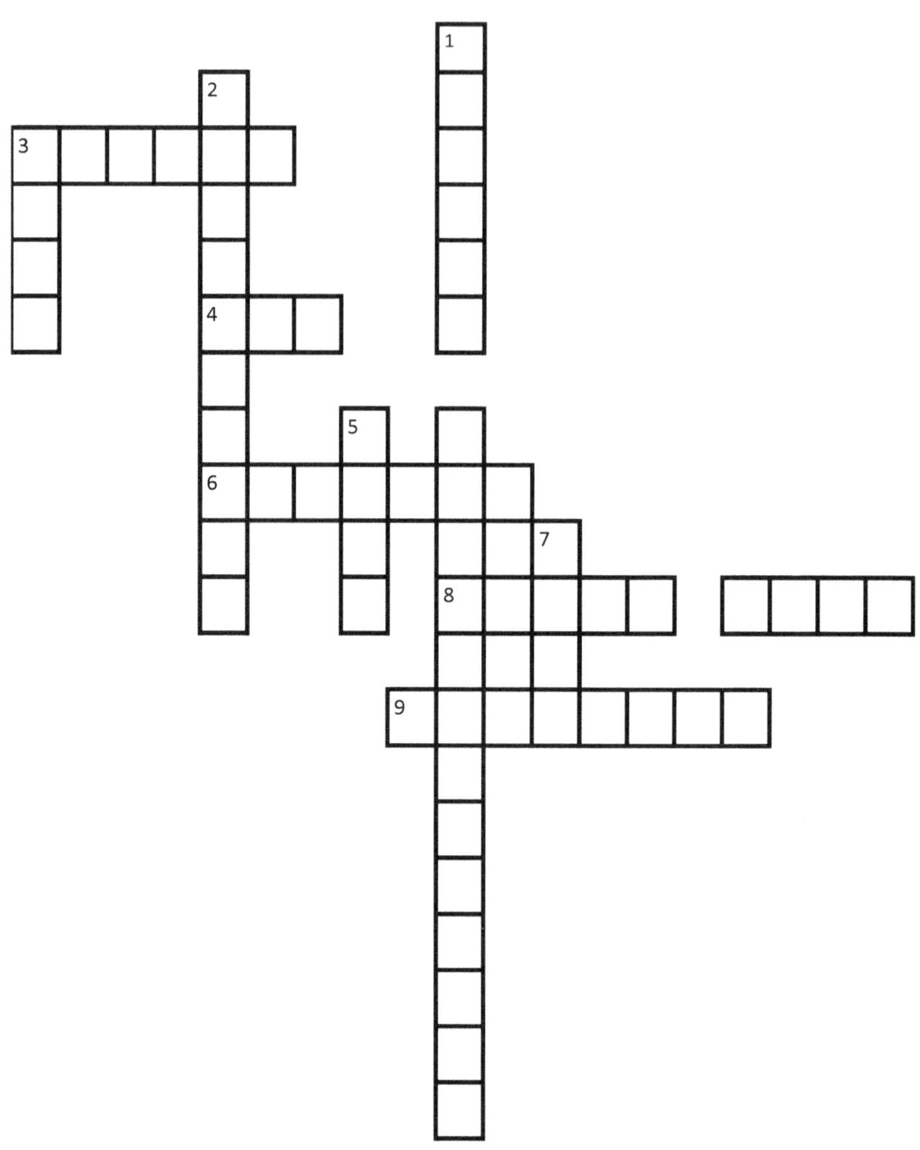

First Timothy

ACROSS

1. An overseer must rule his own house ___________

6. In his church, Timothy served the ___________

8. Chapter 1, verses 12-17 is Paul's ___________

9. Timothy was a __________preacher

10. Elders that rule well should receive ________ ___________ (two-word answer)

DOWN

2. The law is for the __________

3. Fifty-fourth book of the Bible (two-word answer)

4. Overseer or elder

5. Widows should be ___________for by the church

7. Name Timothy means ___________ ________ __________ (three-word answer)

First Timothy

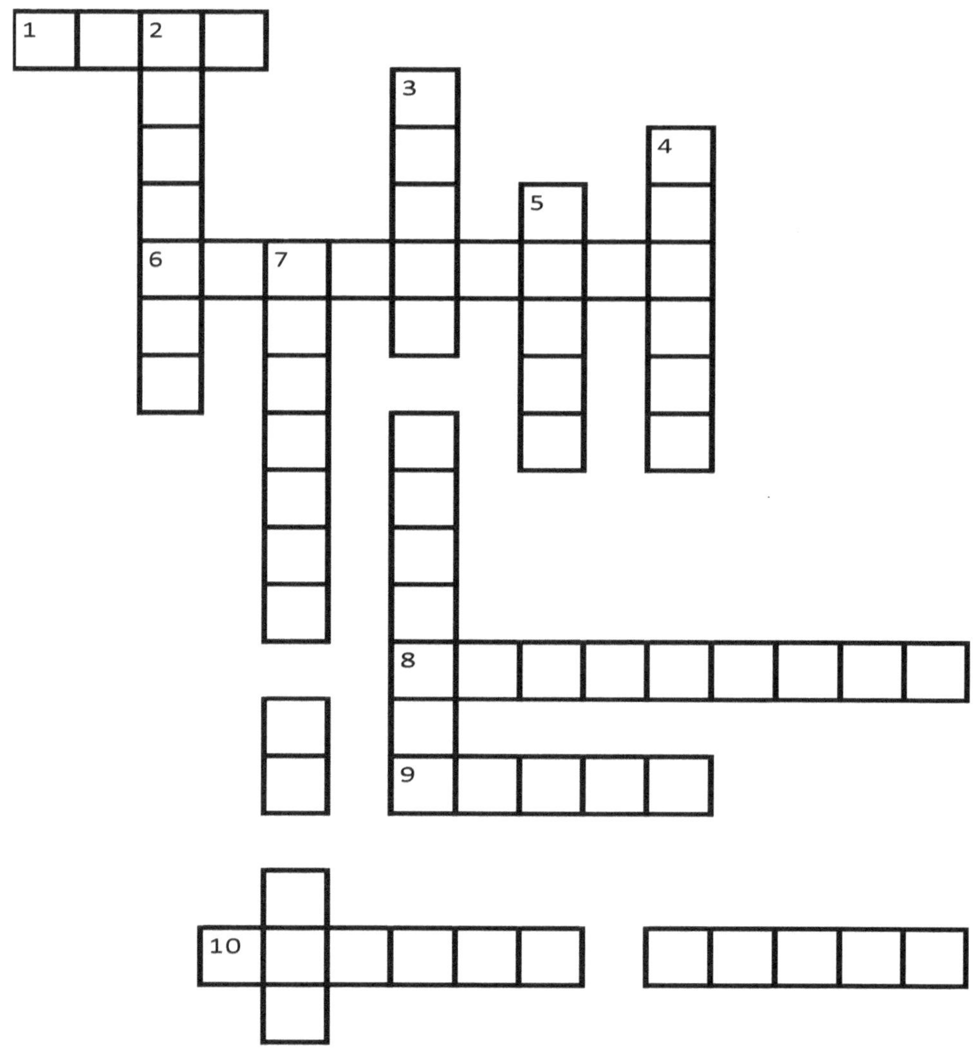

Second Timothy

ACROSS

2. All scripture is given by _________ of God
4. Timothy's father in the gospel
7. Paul sent _____________ to Ephesus
8. Aided Paul in Rome and Ephesus
9. An advisor of Paul
11. First word of the fifty-fifth book of the Bible.
12. _________ remained with Paul after three people left him in Rome
14. Second word of the fifty-fifth book of the Bible

DOWN

1. What Second Timothy 1:12 is to the book as a whole (two-word answer)
3. Friends of Paul (two-word answer)
5. Paul identified himself as an _______ (1:1)
6. Name of Timothy's grandmother
10. Paul requested _________ to come to Rome.
11. Endure hardship as a good ________
13. Timothy's mother

Second Timothy

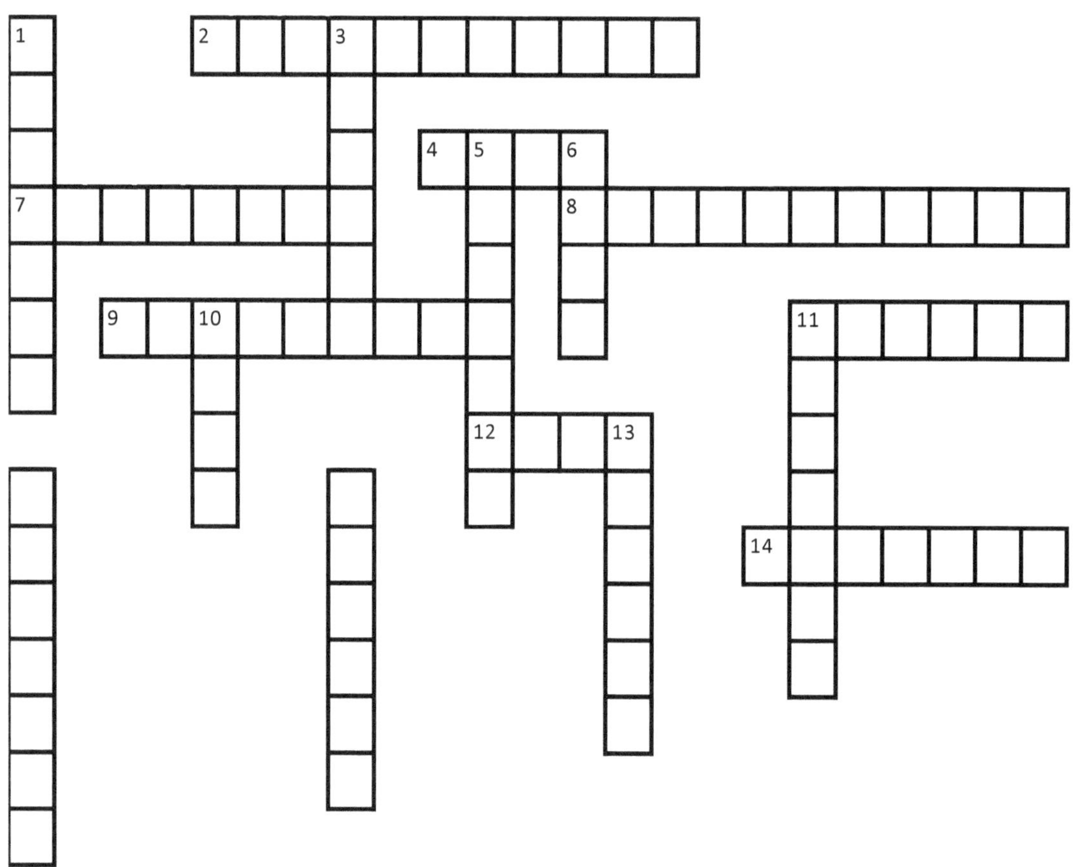

Titus

ACROSS

3. Church should have sound _________

6. Fifty-sixth book of the Bible

8. Reputation of the Cretans

9. A qualification for an elder

10. Titus was Paul's __________

DOWN

1. Titus states the qualifications that an _________ needs

2. Number of chapters in the book

4. Titus was on the island of ________ when he wrote this epistle.

5. Paul spent the winter at this place

7. Young men should have _________ __________

Titus

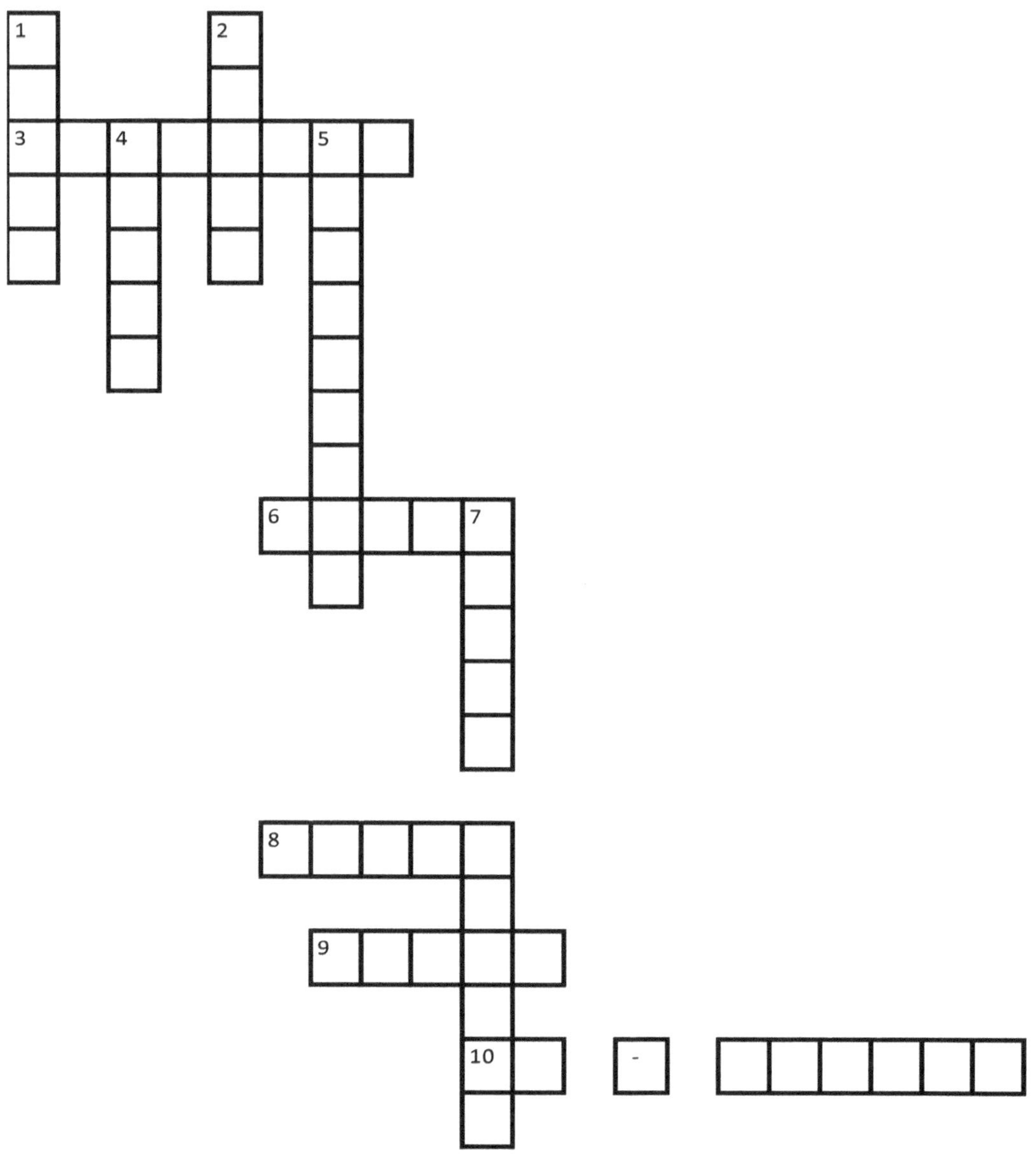

Philemon

ACROSS

1. Fifty-seventh book of the Bible
2. Domestic slave
5. Wife of Philemon
6. Paul promised to pay the entire ________ of Onesimus.
7. Philemon was a ________ ________ and friend of Paul (two-word answer)
9. Number of verses in the book (two-word answer)

DOWN

1. Meaning of Onesimus
3. Fellow prisoner
4. What the message "Put that on my account" is to the entire book (two-word answer)
8. Onesimus left Philemon a sinner and returned a "________ beloved"___

Philemon

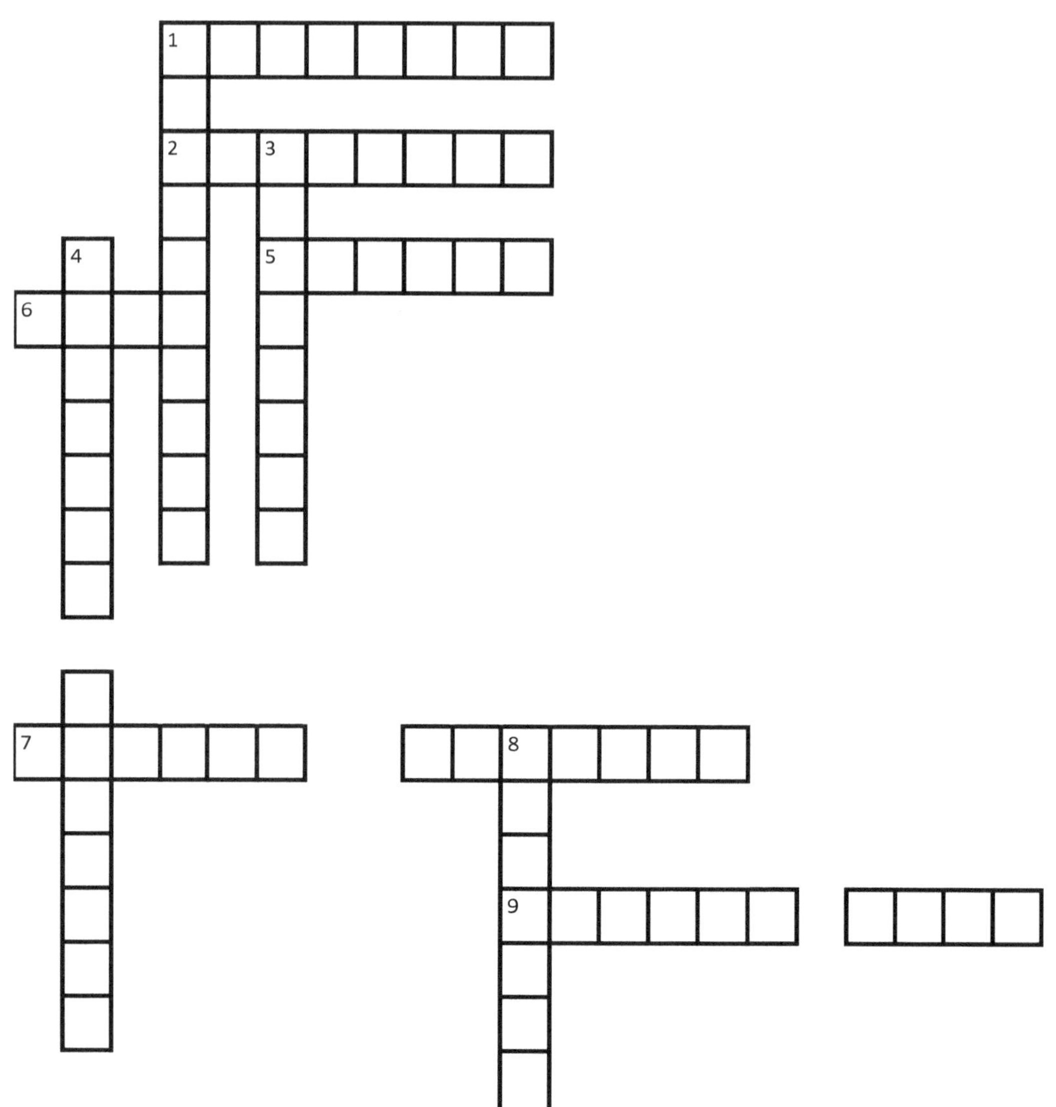

Hebrews

ACROSS

2. Fifty-eighth book of the Bible
3. Things hoped for, evidence of things not seen
7. Old covenant (two-word answer)
9. New covenant (two-word answer)
11. "__________ is mine, I will repay" said the Lord.
13. Lay aside every ___________

DOWN

1. King of Salem and priest
3. He will not leave you or __________ you
4. Jesus is our High Priest on the ________ _______ of the father (two-word answer)
5. He was taken away and did not see death.
6. The _______shall live by faith
8. Highest priest forever (two-word answer)
10. City of God (two-word answer)
12. By faith, _________ prepared the ark.

Hebrews

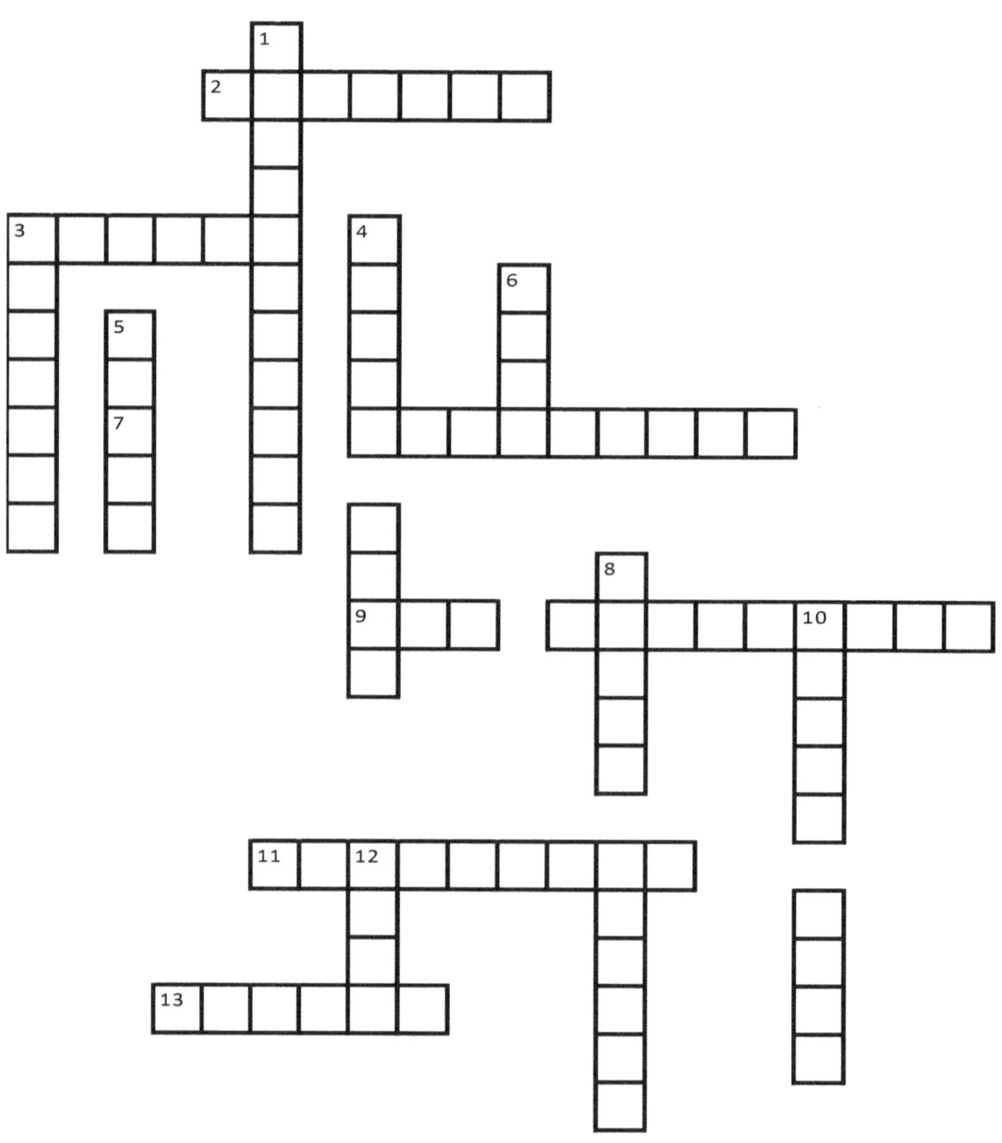

James

ACROSS

3. Isaac's father

6. A person should be swift to hear and _________ to speak

7. Resist the devil, and he will _______

9. Love your neighbor as ___________

12. A harlot

13. Let your yes be _______ and your no be _______

14. __________ comes from God. Ask God for ___________ (two-word answer)

DOWN

1. Faith without works is ___________

2. Fifty-ninth book of the Bible

4. __________faults one to another

5. James wrote this epistle to the __________ __________

8. Dynamic instrument

10. To overcome sin, one must _______ to God.

11. Be doers of the _________

James

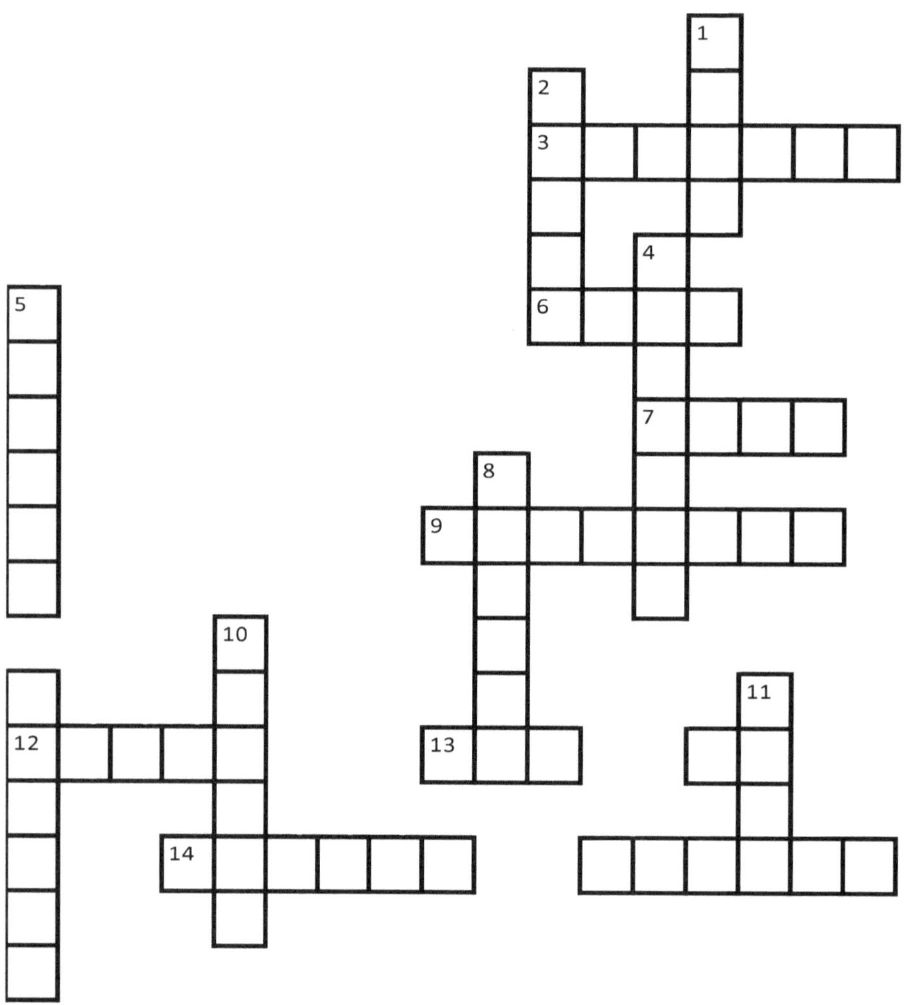

First Peter

ACROSS

3. Resist the __________

6. Peter's original name

7. Have __________one for another.

9. Do not return evil for __________

10. Put aside __________

DOWN

1. Should be submissive to their master

2. Sixtieth book of the Bible

4. Should give honor to wives

5. the name Peter means _________ _________ __________

7. Example for Christians

8. Wife of Abraham

First Peter

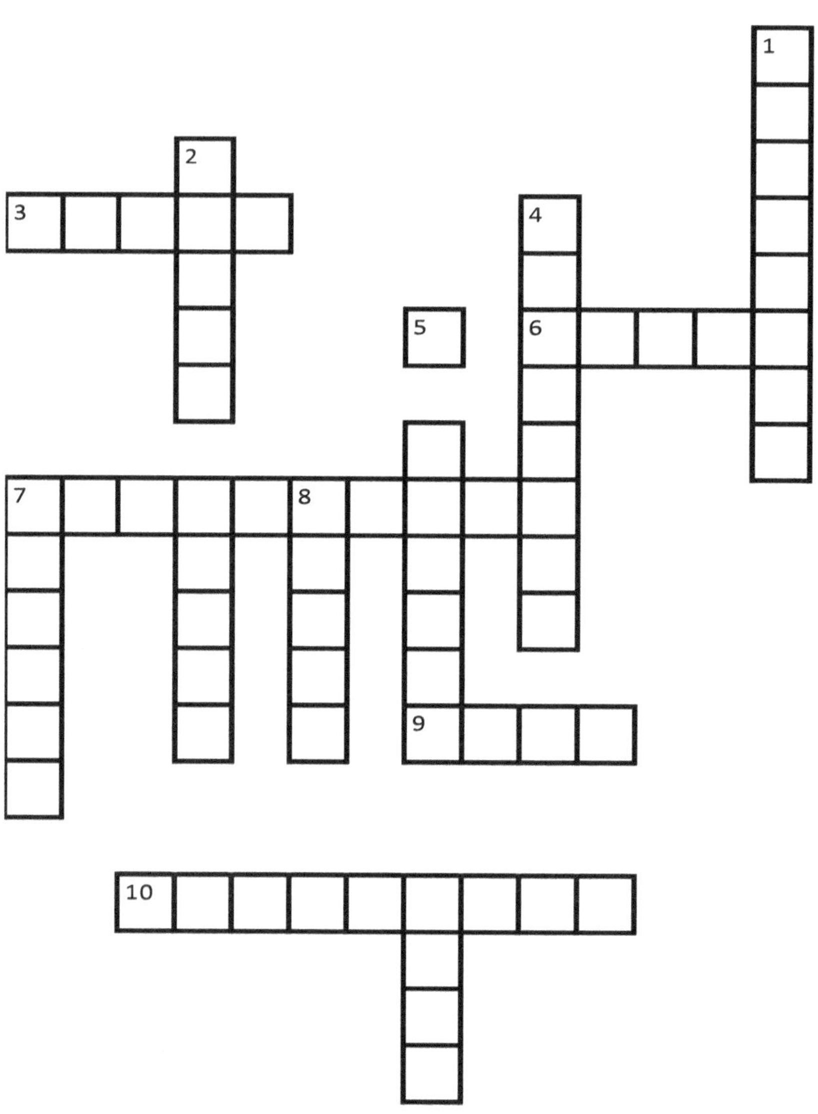

Second Peter

ACROSS

4. A city that was turned to ashes by God

5. This preacher of righteousness built an ark

7. the Lord will come as a __________ in the night

9. Teachers of righteousness (two-word answer)

DOWN

1. Peter warns against false teachers and false ________

2. Holy men of God are moved by the ______ ________ (two-word answer)

3. One day with the Lord is as a _______ years

6. Sixty-first book of the Bible (two-word answer)

8. One should add ____________ to brotherly kindness

Second Peter

First John

ACROSS

2. Love one ____________

5. Whoever hates his brother is a ______

7. These words are the central message of the book and appear over thirty times (two-word answer)

9. Confessing sins brings ____________

10. The book pits love versus hatred, truth versus error, and light versus _______

DOWN

1. All sinners have _______ ________as an advocate with the Father (two-word answer)

3. Perfect love casts out ___________

4. Sixty-second book of the Bible (two-word answer)

6. Whoever is born of God does not ___________

8. John warns Christians to "Love not the ____________"

First John

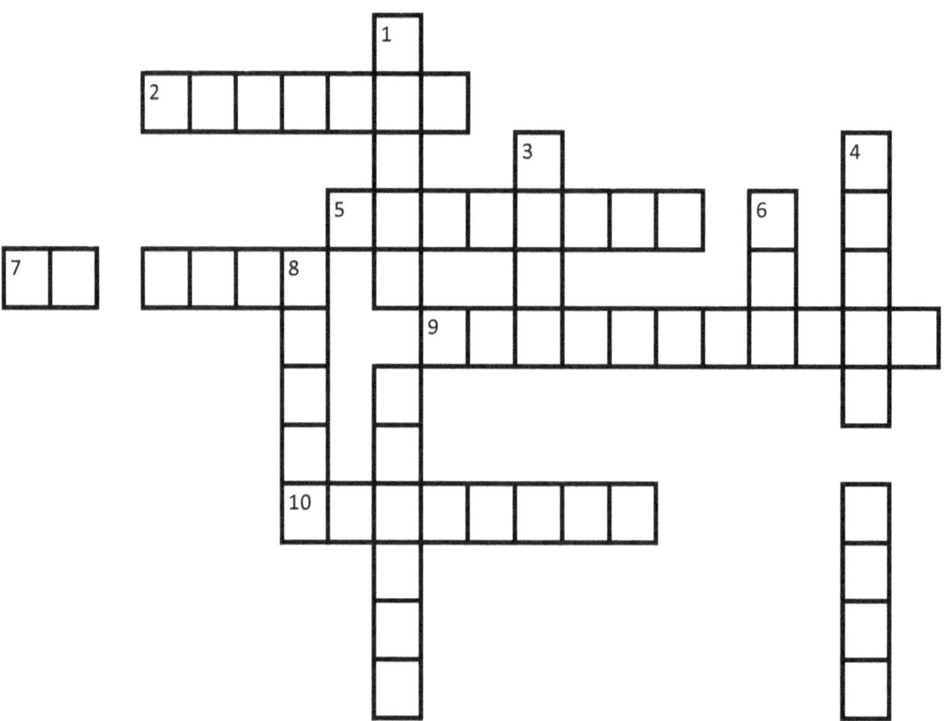

Second John

ACROSS

1. John is identified as an __________

3. Do not receive __________into your home.

6. Love one _________is a commandment from the Father

DOWN

1. This letter was written to an ______ ________ (two-word answer)

2. _________, mercy, and peace come from God

4. Sixty-third book of the Bible (two-word answer)

5. Those who do not confess Christ

Second John

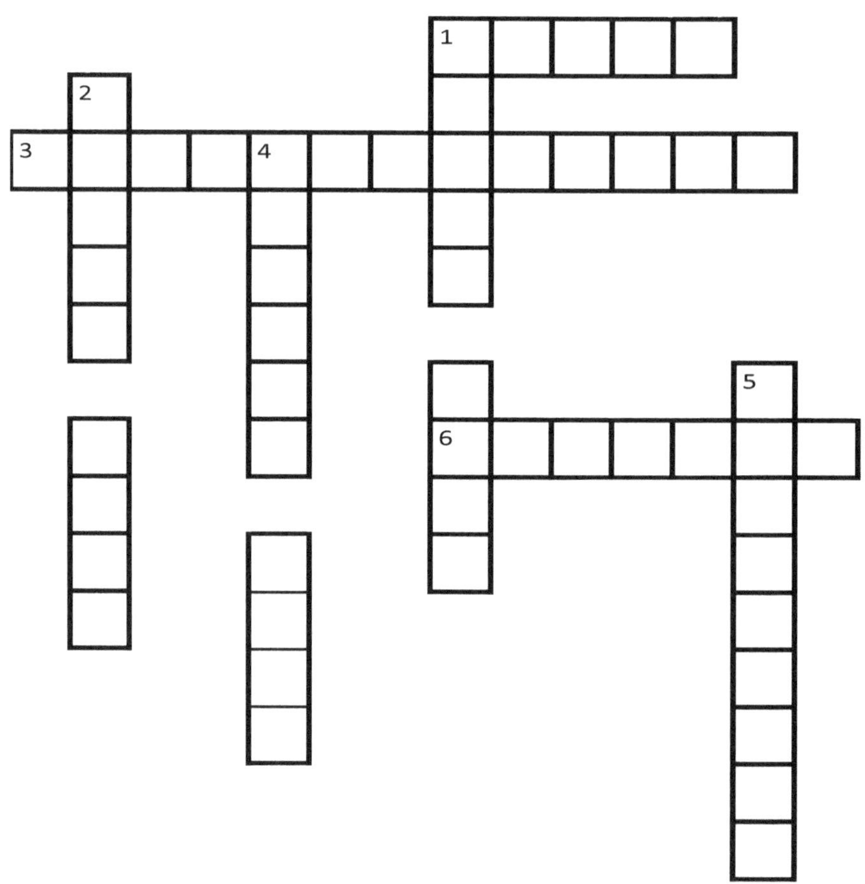

Third John

ACROSS

3. Do not imitate ________

6. Sixty-fourth book of the Bible (two-word answer)

7. This man is highly recommended by his friends and by the truth itself

8. This book was written to _________

DOWN

1. John called Gaius "the _________" four times

2. Spoke malicious statements against John

4. John prayed for Gaius to ________in all things.

5. Gaius was a man of __________

Third John

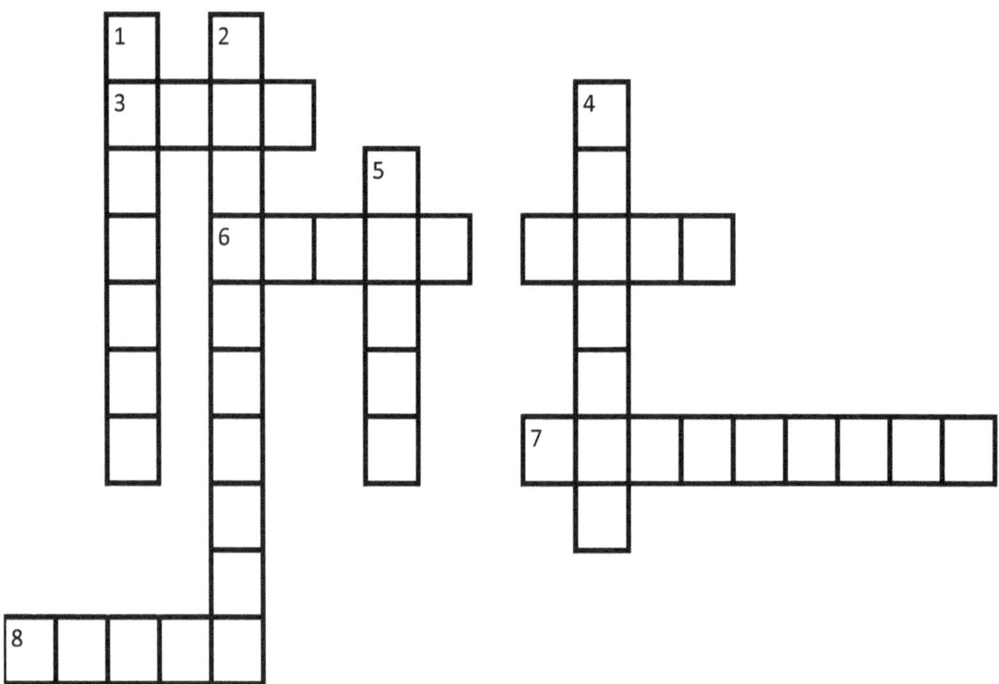

Jude

ACROSS

2. Strive for the ___________which was delivered unto the Saints.

3. Seventh from Adam

5. Sixty-fifth book of the Bible

6. The Lord saved Israel out of the land of __________

9. These ________ ________ denied Jesus Christ (two-word answer)

DOWN

1. Archangel

4. Number of chapters in this book

5. The Lord will execute ___________

7. Son of Adam and Eve; he killed his brother

Jude

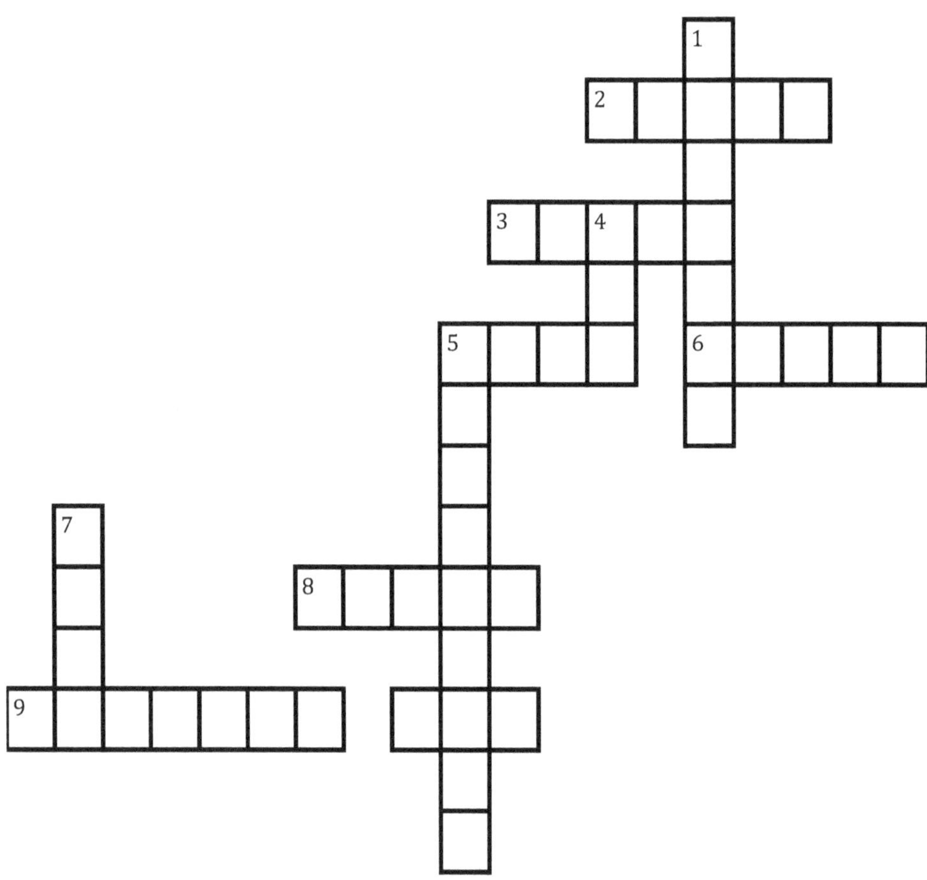

Revelation

ACROSS

3. The dead church

5. The fifth bowl represents __________ and pain.

7. Blessed are the dead who die in the _______________

8. Jezebel committee sexual acts while teaching in the church in this city.

10. The mother of harlots (three-word answer)

12. Sixty-sixth book of the Bible

14. John saw a multitude which no man could _________

15. The faithful church

17. Means to unveil or reveal

18. 144,000 were without faults before the throne of ___________

19. Worthy is the __________

DOWN

1. He who sat on a white horse

2. Chapter 1, verse 1, is the _______ _________ of this book (two-word answer)

4. Seven churches were located in __________

6. It was cast out of heaven (two-word answer)

9. Four living creatures said "Holy, Holy, Holy, ________ ________ ________" (three-word answer)

11. John is told to eat _________ ________ _________ (three-word answer)

13. Number of chapters in this book (two-word answer)

16. If anyone has an ear, let him _______

17. Beginning and end (two-word answer)

Revelation

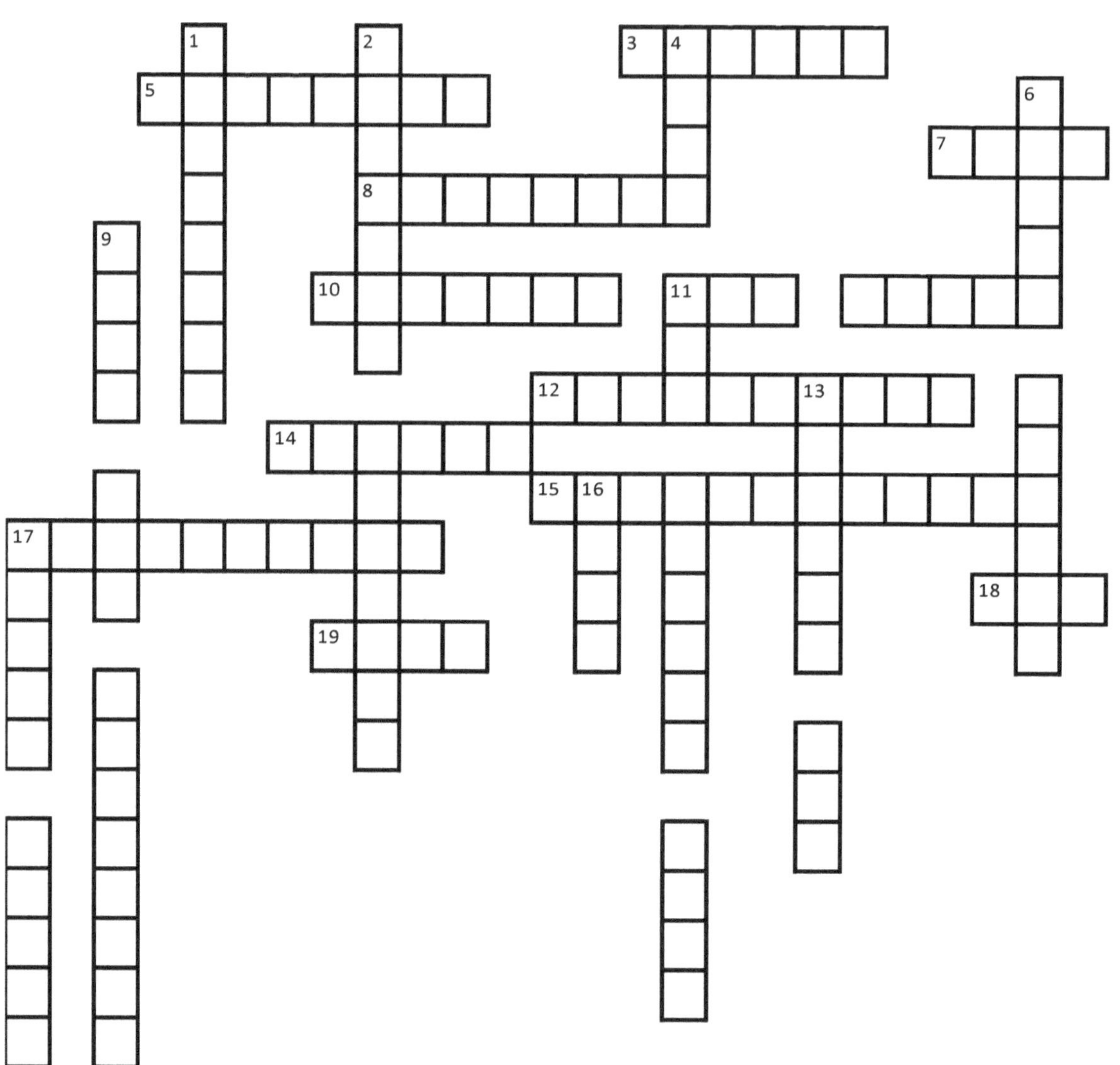

Twenty-Seven Bible Crosswords
Answers

Matthew

1 GOD
2 FORTY
TWO
3 TWELVE
4 PETER
5 JESSE
6 WOE
7 THIRTY
8 BETHLEHEM
9 LOVE
10 MATTHEW
HIMSELF
11 TAX
COLLECTOR
12 TWO
13 MASTERS
MOUNT
OF
OLIVES
14 SADDUCEES
15 AMEN
16 PRAYER
17 THEME
THREE
18 CENTURION
19 ZEBEDEE
20 JUDAS
ISCARIOT

Mark

1 ZEBEDEE
2 MARK
2 MARY
3 TEMPLE
3 TWELVE
4 BARABBAS
5 GETHSEMANE
6 FOOTSTOOL
7 SYNOPTIC
8 CAESAR
9 JOSEPH
9 JUDAS
10 SABBATH
11 PETER
12 BLIND
13 LEPER
BARTIMAEUS
14 REPENTANCE
15 JORDAN
16 SADDUCEES
ISCARIOT
17 GOLGOTHA

Luke

1 P I L A T E
2 S I M O N
3 S O N O F D A V I D
3 S A D D U C E E S
4 C H I L D R E N
5 B E T H L E H E M
6 L U K E
7 L A Z A R U S
8 S Y N A G O G U E
9 P A S S O V E R
9 P R I E S T
10 S I M E O N
11 H E R O D
12 E L I Z A B E T H
13 W I D O W
14 J E R U S A L E M
15 W E P T
16 D E N I E D
17 P O N T I U S P I L A T E
18 G A B R I E L

John

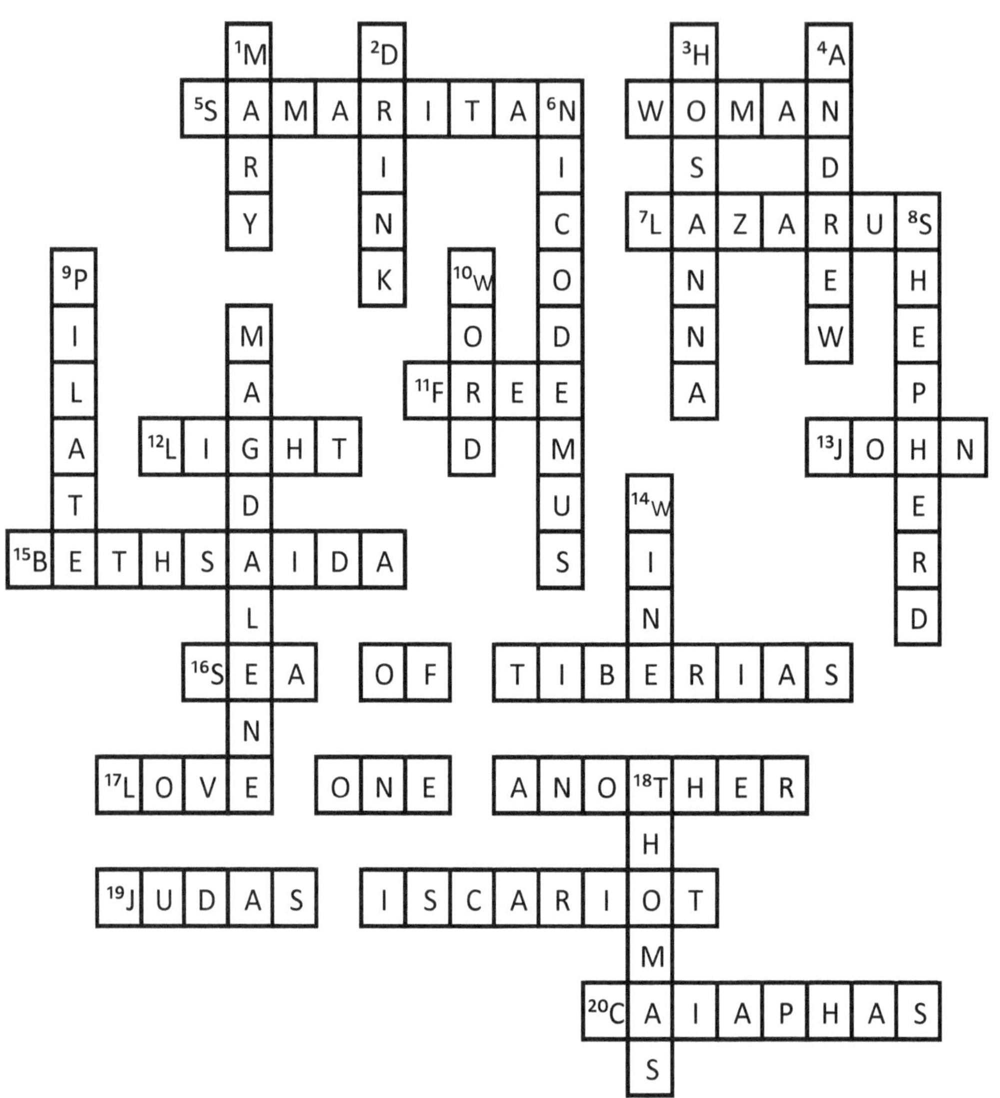

Acts

Romans

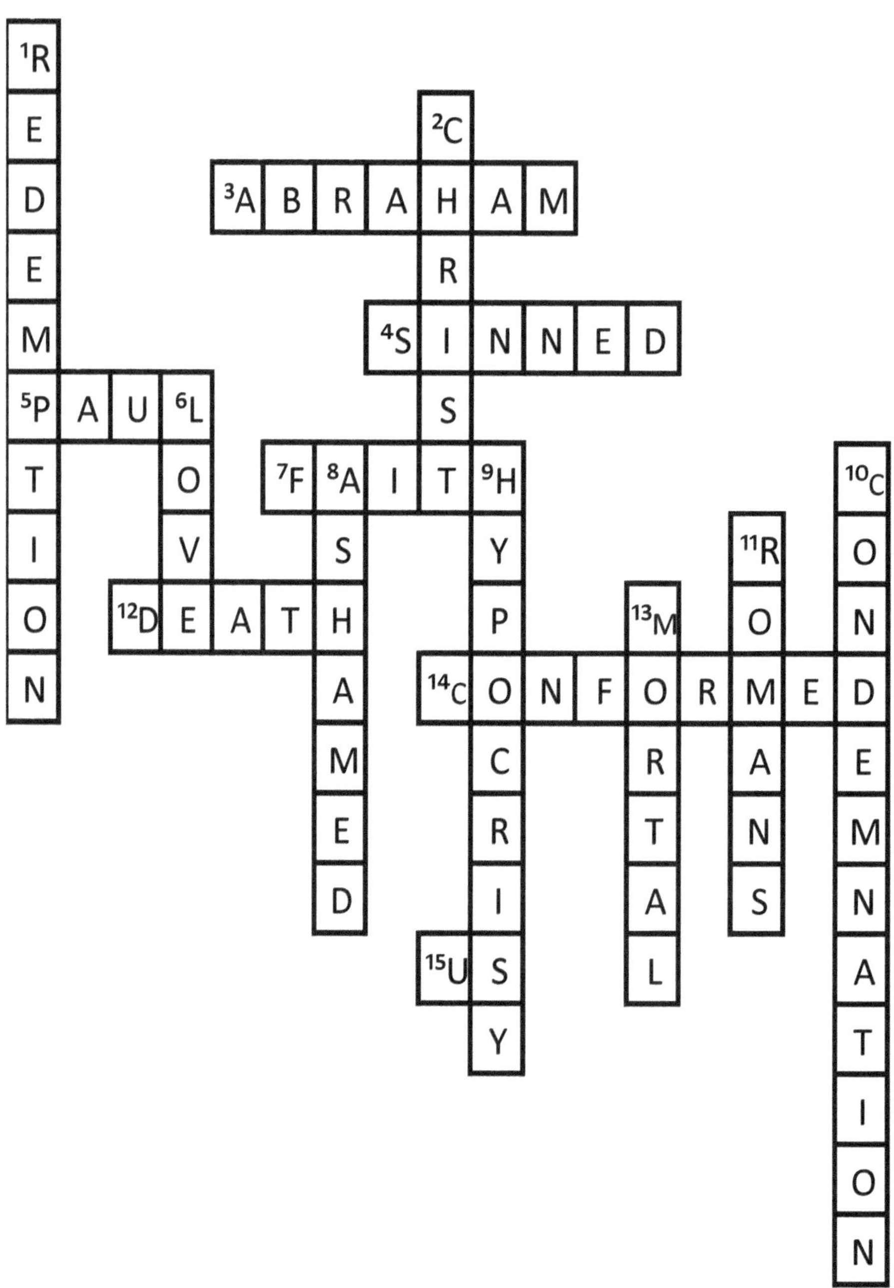
1 REDEMPTION
2 CHRIST
3 ABRAHAM
4 SINNED
5 PAUL
6 LOVE
7 FAITH
8 ASHAMED
9 HYPOCRISY
10 CONDEMNATION
11 ROMANS
12 DEATH
13 MORTAL
14 CONFORMED
15 US

First Corinthians

Second Corinthians

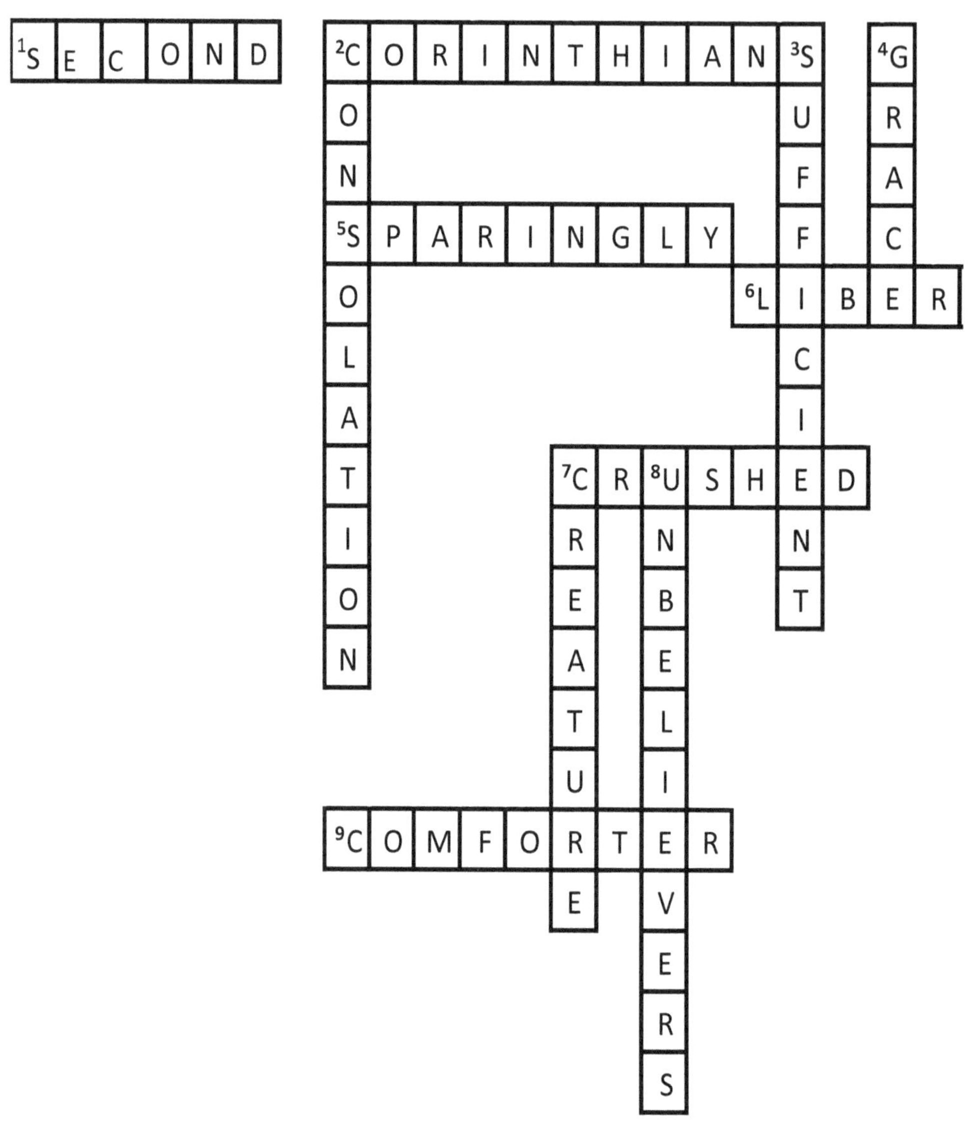

Galatians

1 LIVES
2 GALATIANS
3 JAMES
4 JESUS
5 PETER
6 BURDENS
BARNABAS
7 BONDSERVANT
8 DAYS
9 YOURSELF
10 WALK
11 FAITH
12 CENTRAL
CHRIST
MESSAGE

Ephesians

1K
2A
3IMITATORS
4C
5HILDREN
UMD
6SIX
BOR
A
7W
8M
N
9LIGHT
E
D
V
10PRIS
11ONER
C
N
S
12M
13ERCY
E
P
H
E
O
14SIN
N
I
15EPHESUS
A
N
S

Philippians

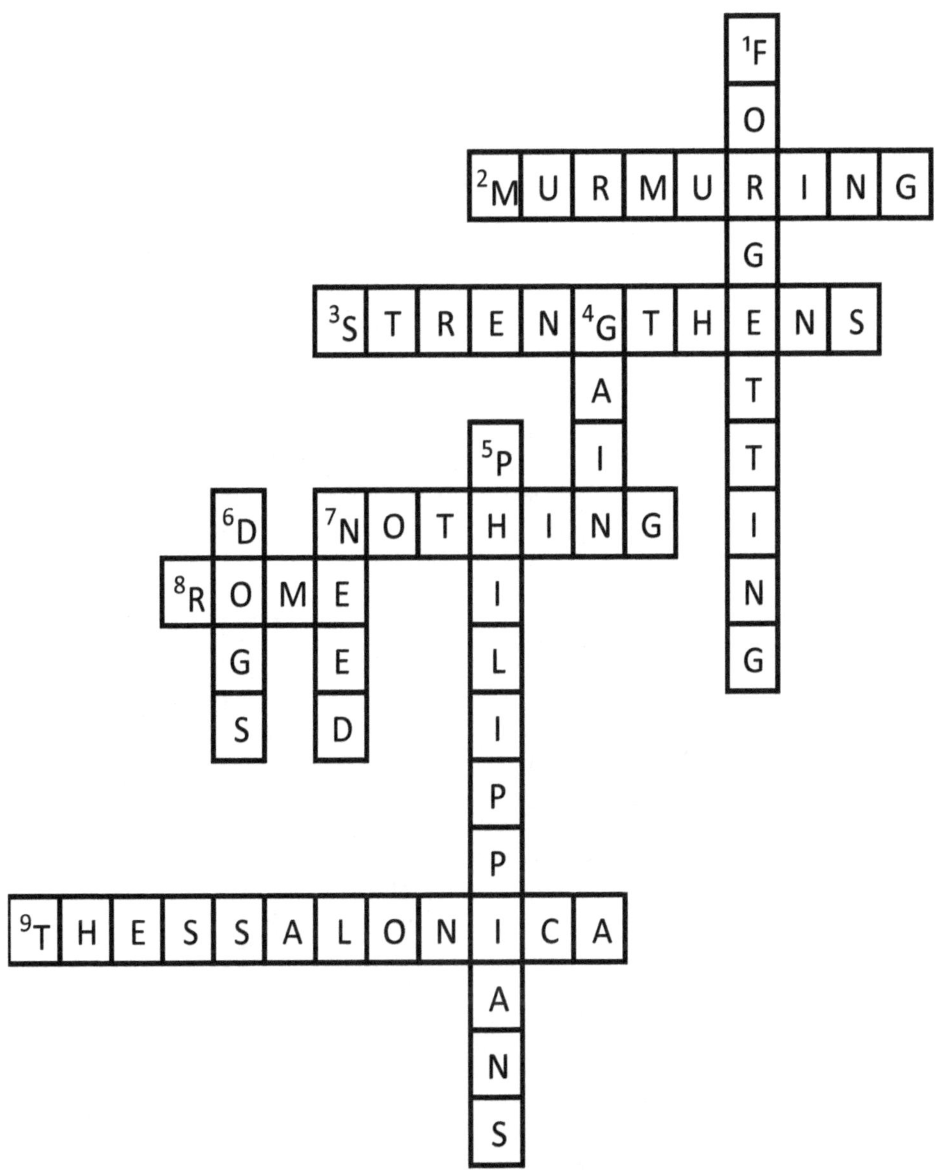

Colossians

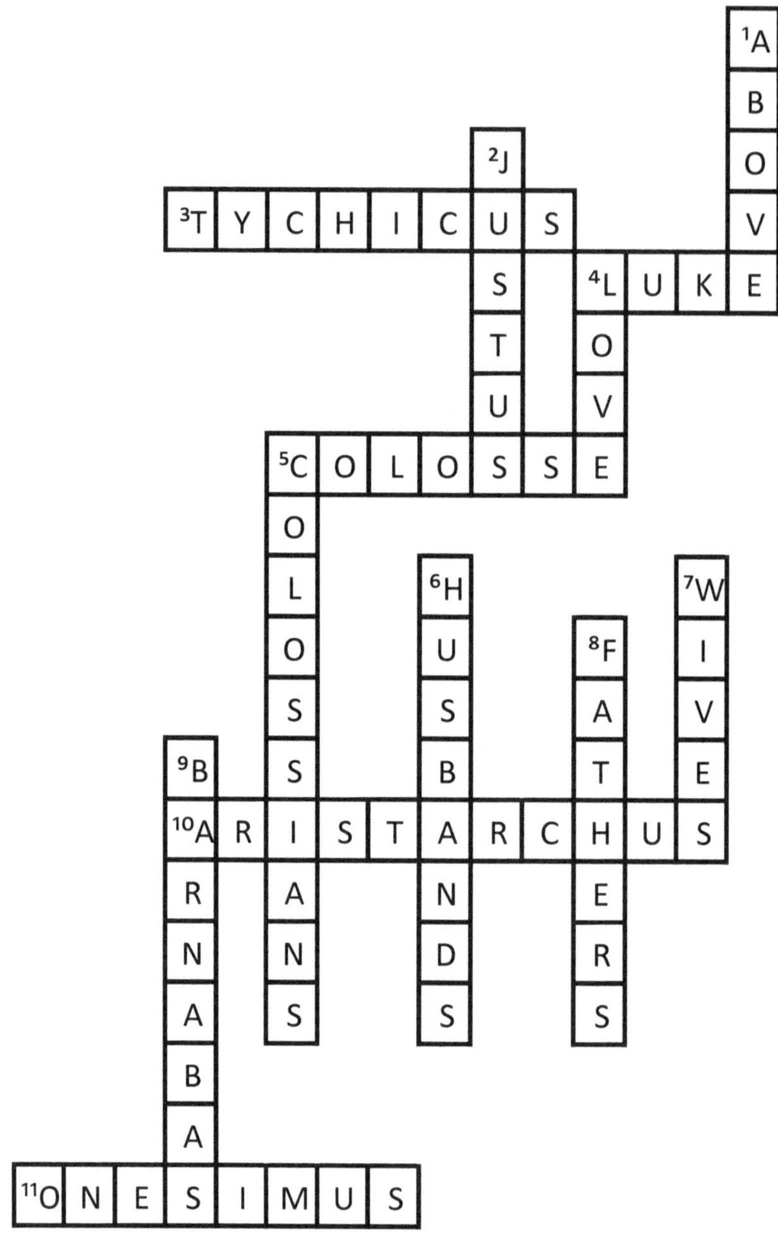

1 ABOVE
2 JUSTUS
3 TYCHICUS
4 LUKE
4 LOVE
5 COLOSSE
5 COLOSSIANS
6 HUSBANDS
7 WIVES
8 FATHERS
9 BARNABA
10 ARISTARCHUS
11 ONESIMUS

First Thessalonians

Second Thessalonians

First Timothy

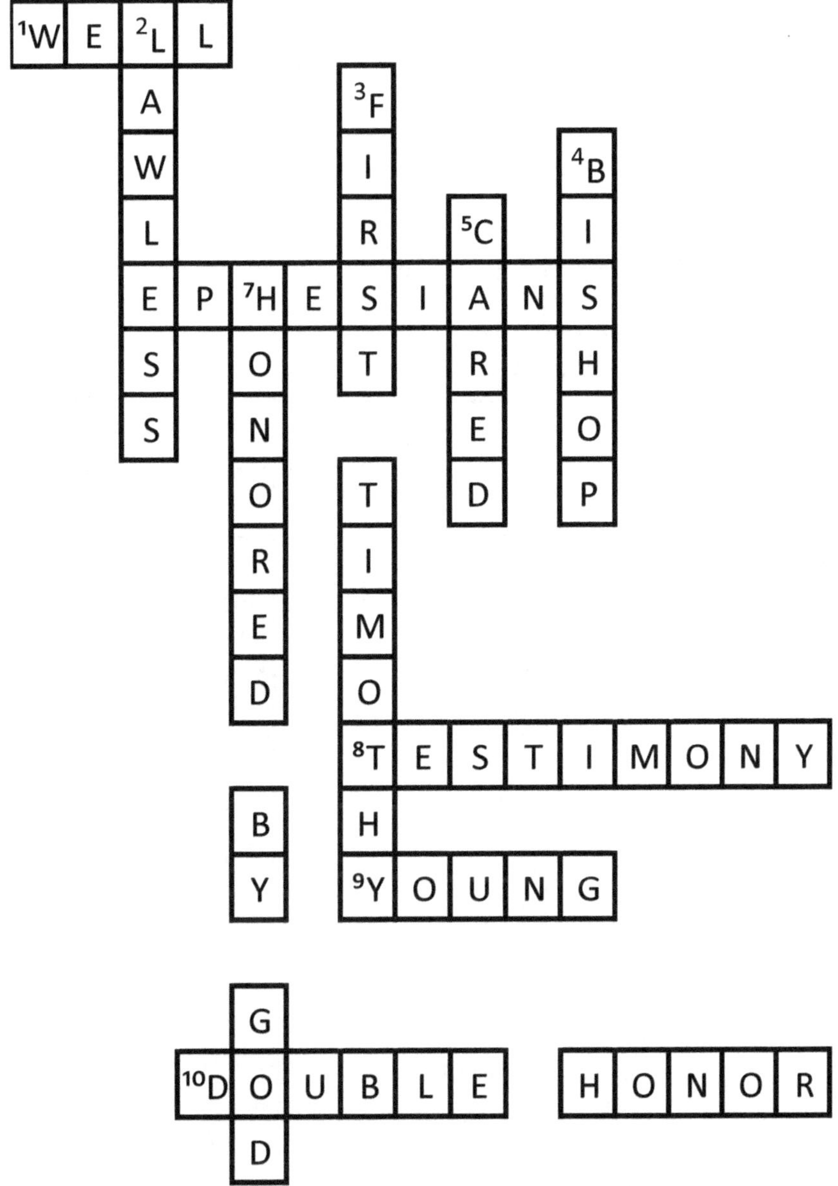

Second Timothy

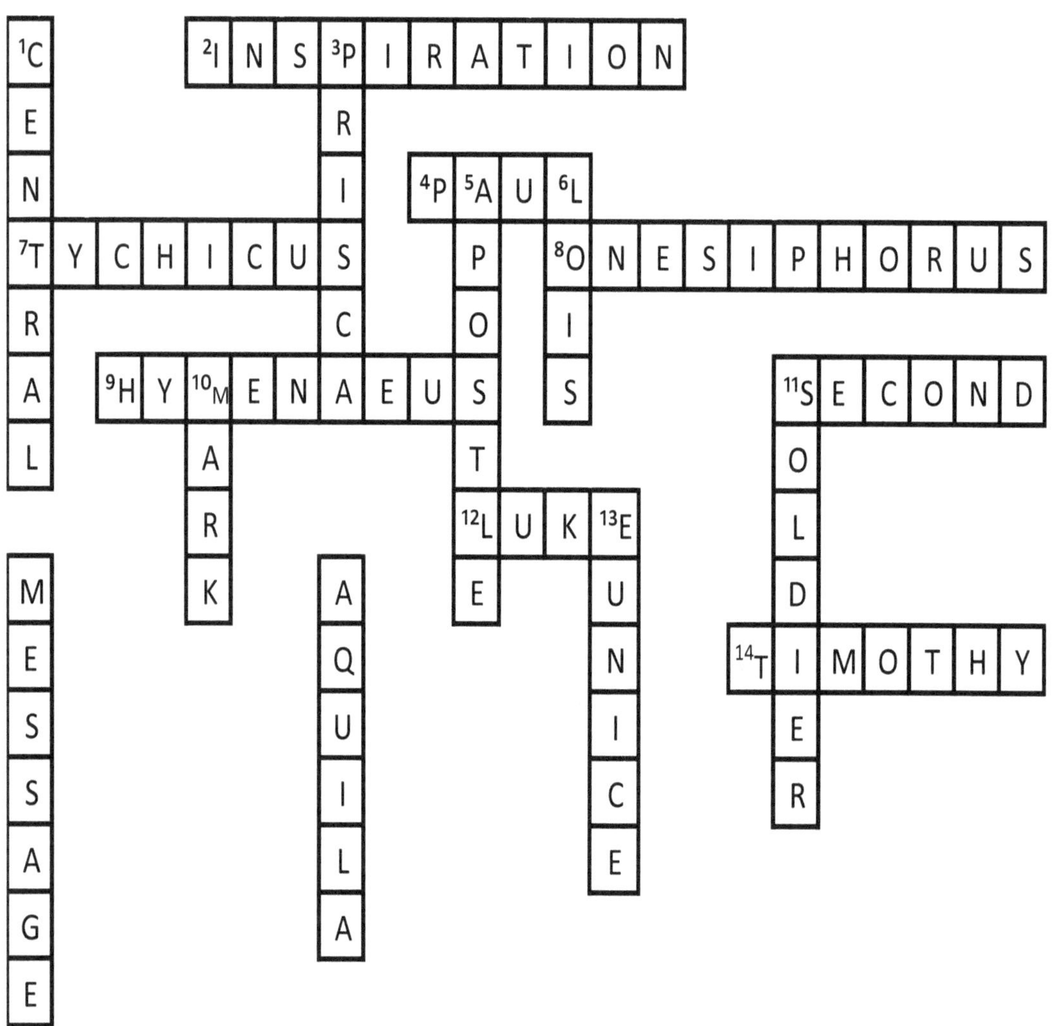

Titus

Philemon

1 PHILEMON
2 ONESIMUS
3 EPAPHRAS
4 CENTRAL
5 APPHIA
6 DEBT
PROFITABLE
7 FELLOW
MESSAGE
LABORER
8 BROTHER
9 TWENTY FIVE

Hebrews

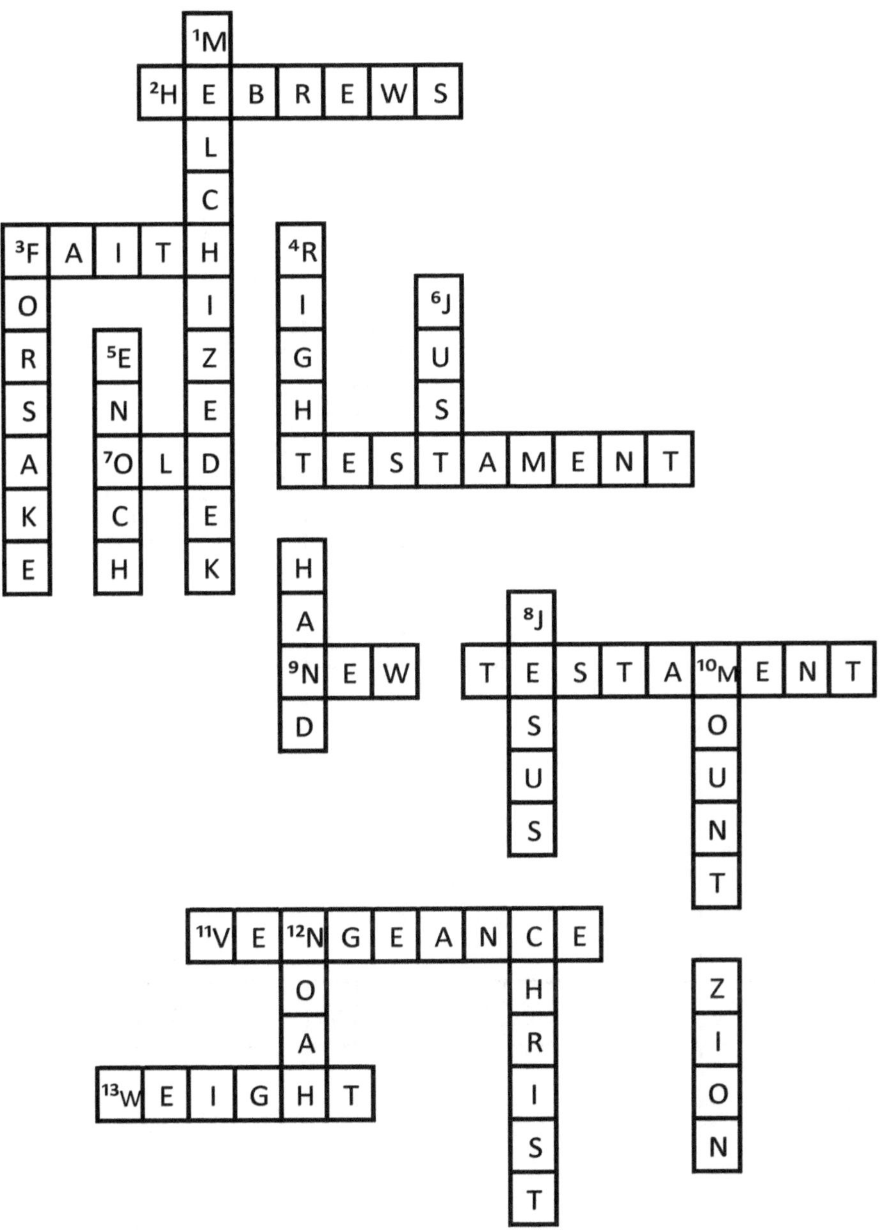

James

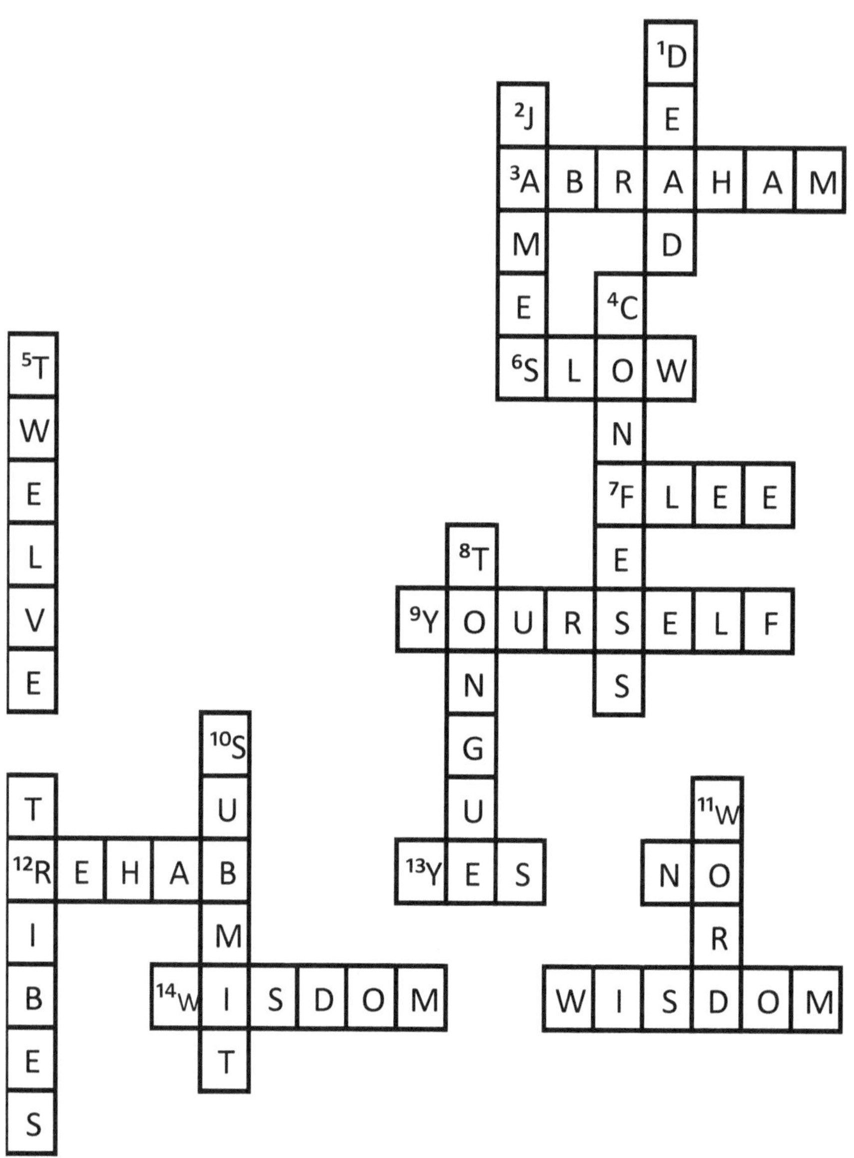

1 D E A D
2 J A M E S
3 A B R A H A M
4 C O N F E S S
5 T W E L V E
6 S L O W
7 F L E E
8 T O N G U E
9 Y O U R S E L F
10 S U B M I T
11 W O R D
12 R E H A B
13 Y E S
14 W I S D O M
T R I B E S
N O
W I S D O M

First Peter

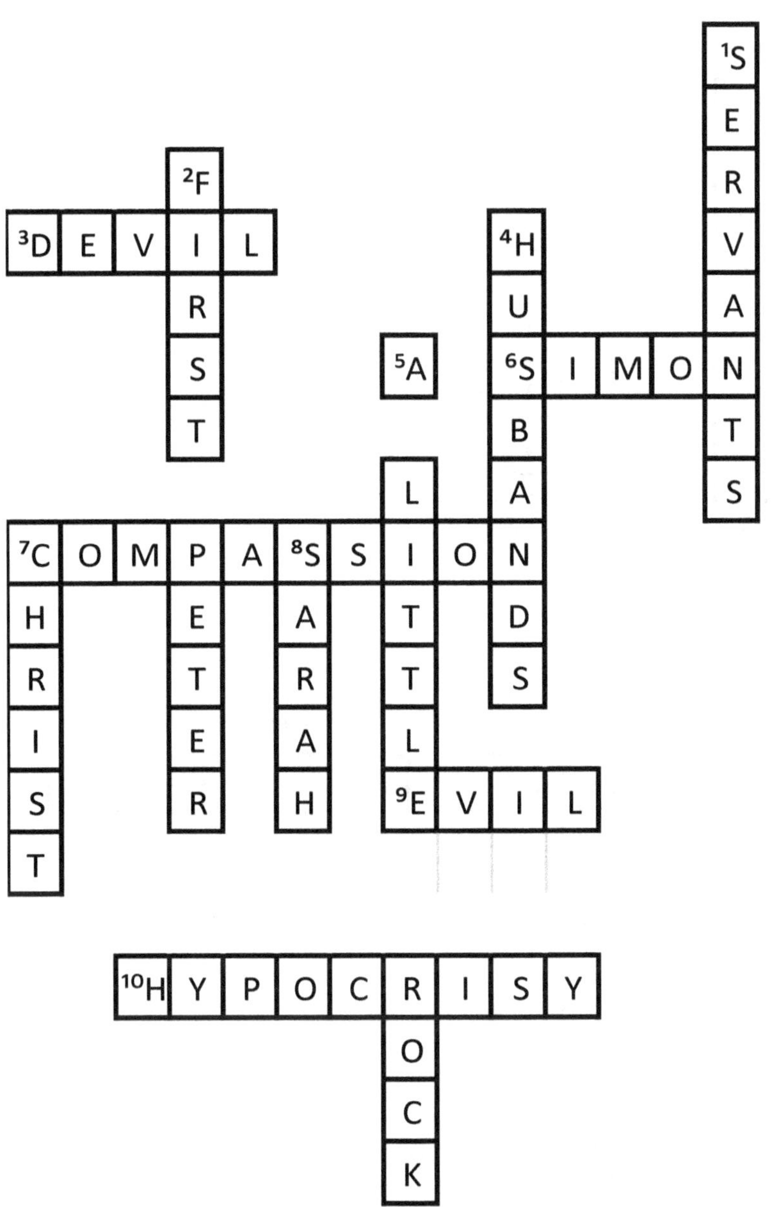
1 SERVANTS
2 FIRST
3 DEVIL
4 HUSBANDS
5 ALITTLE
6 SIMON
7 COMPASSION
7 CHRIST
8 SARAH
PETER
9 EVIL
10 HYPOCRISY
ROCK

Second Peter

First John

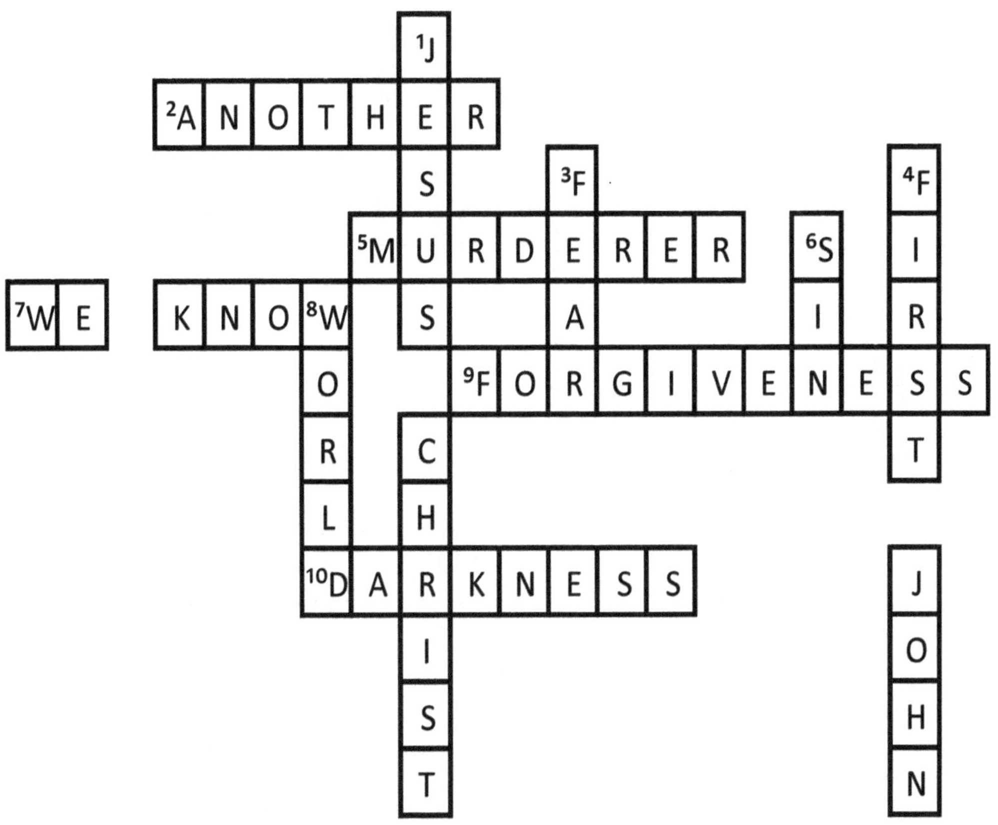

1 JESUS CHRIST
2 ANOTHER
3 FEAR
4 FIRST JOHN
5 MURDERER
6 SIN
7 WE KNOW
8 WORLD
9 FORGIVENESS
10 DARKNESS

Second John

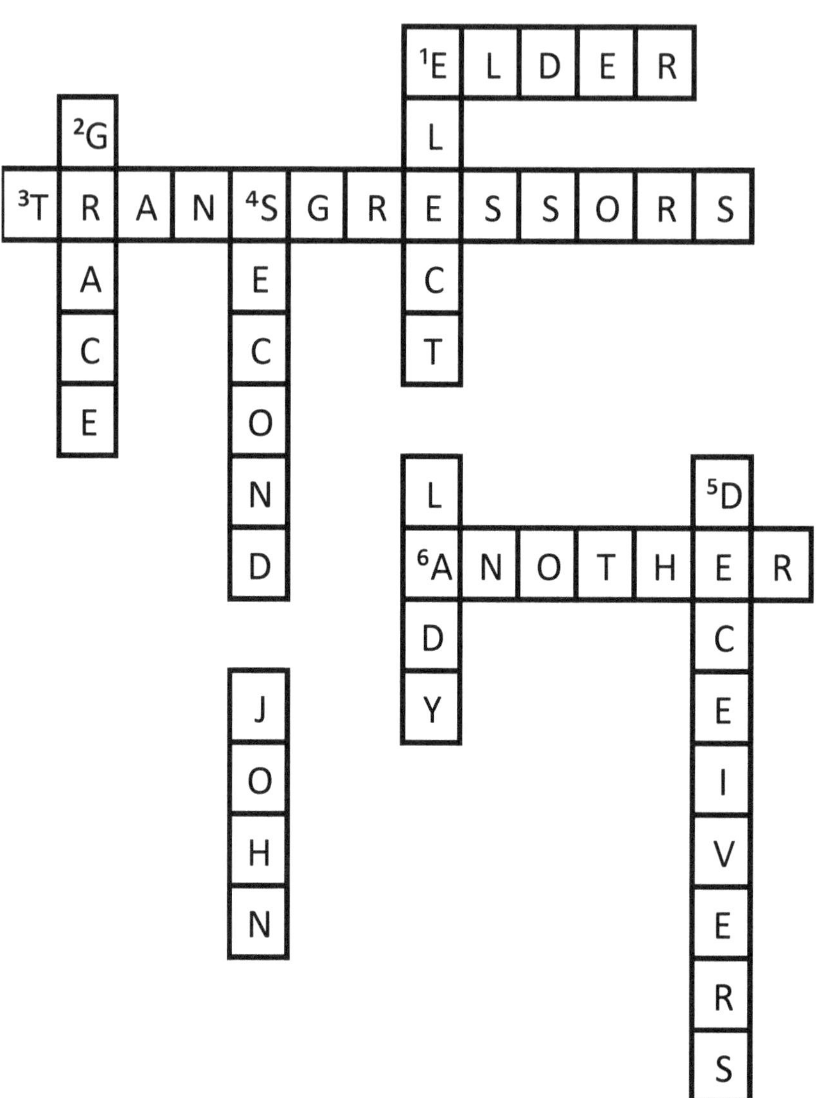
1 ELDER
ELECT
2 GRACE
3 TRANSGRESSORS
4 SECOND
JOHN
LADY
5 DECEIVERS
6 ANOTHER

Third John

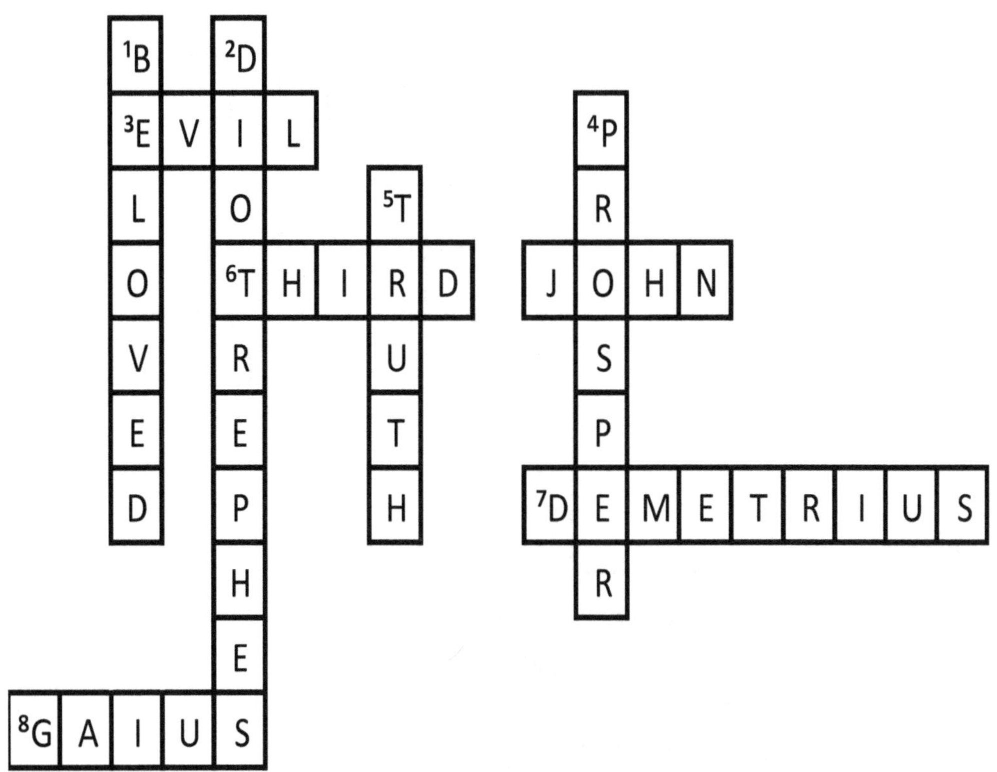

1 BELOVED
2 DIOTREPHES
3 EVIL
4 PROSPER
5 TRUTH
6 THIRD
JOHN
7 DEMETRIUS
8 GAIUS

Jude

1 MICHAEL
2 FAITH
3 ENOCH
4 ONE
5 JUDE
5 JUDGEMENT
6 EGYPT
7 CAIN
8 JAMES
9 UNGODLY
MEN

Revelation

1 FAITHFUL
2 CENTERAL
3 SARDIS
4 ASIA
5 DARKNESS
6 GREAT
7 LORD
8 THYATIRA
9 LORD
10 BABYLON
11 THE
GREAT
12 REVELATION
13 TWENTY
TWO
14 NUMBER
15 PHILADELPHIA
16 HEAR
17 APOCALYPSE
18 GOD
19 LAMB
GOD
ALPHA
OMEGA
ALMIGHTY
MESSAGE
LITTLE
BOOK
DRAGON

About the Author

Bernard Kent, Jr. was born in Savannah Georgia and graduated from Savannah State College in 1965 with a Bachelor's Degree in Chemistry and Biology. He later attended Warner Pacific College and graduated Cum Laude in 1978 with a Master's of Religion Degree. On August 11, 2000, he received a Doctor of Religious Education Degree from Covington Theological Seminary from which he again graduated Cum Laude.

Dr. Kent has received numerous awards and accolades including: Who's Who Among American Teachers, and Teacher of the Year for Effingham County Public Schools. He is actively involved with the Savannah Church of God where he has been a member for many years.

Dr. Kent is the oldest of three children born to Reverend Bernard Kent, Sr. and Mrs. Ludene Kent. He has two sisters, Mrs. Elise Green and Mrs. Bettie Cannon. Bernard is the father of four children: Schenterial, Sharnda, Absolon, and Berneta. He also has eight grandchildren: Jasmine, Brittany, BreAnna, Alberto, Trenton, Mileak, Malcolm and Matthios (Matty).

Twenty-seven Bible Crosswords is Dr. Kent's second published book. His first book, *Forgiveness: A Process, Not an Act*, was published in 2008.

www.ingramcontent.com/pod-product-compliance
Lightning Source LLC
LaVergne TN
LVHW061220060426
835508LV00014B/1383

9780982353332